© 2024 Sunbird Books, an imprint of Phoenix International Publications, Inc.
8501 West Higgins Road   34 Seymour Street   Heimhuder Straße 81
Chicago, Illinois 60631   London W1H 7JE   20148 Hamburg

www.SunbirdKidsBooks.com

Library of Congress Control Number: 2023943683

ISBN: 978-1-5037-6985-4 Printed in China

IT'S HER STORY

BILLIE JEAN KING

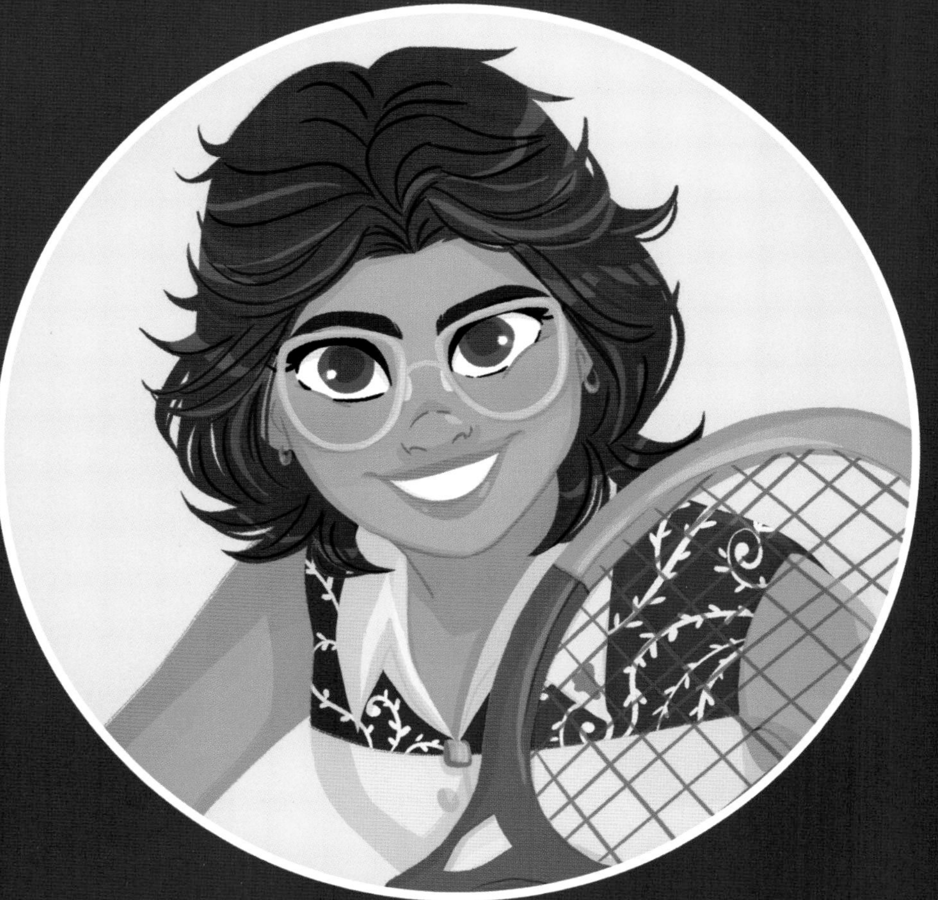

Written by Donna Tapellini
Illustrated by Maria Lia Malandrino

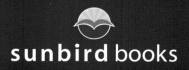

sunbird books

Billie Jean King

had played a lot of tennis matches by the time she was thirty. It was her job, after all. But this match...this match was different.

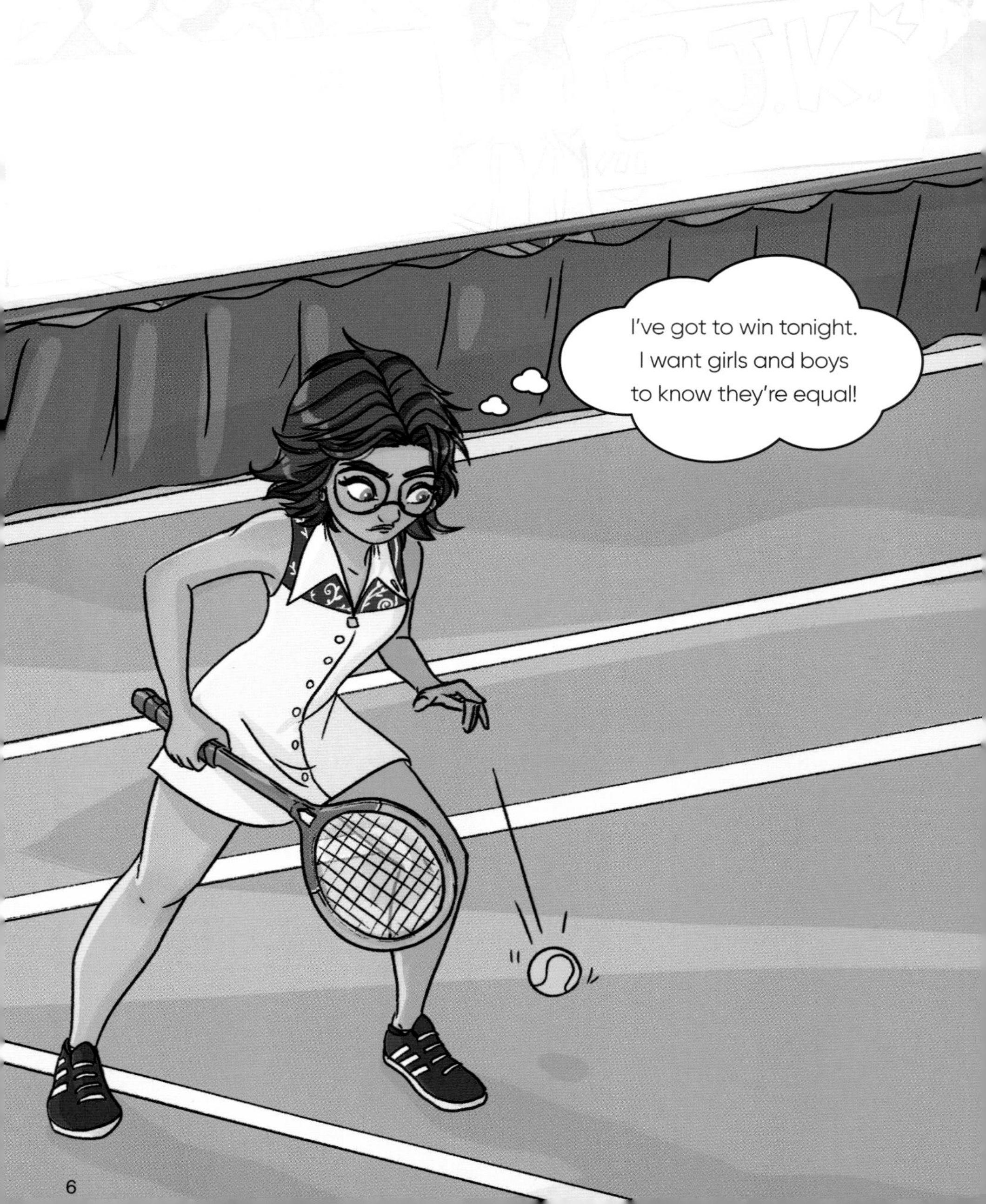
I've got to win tonight. I want girls and boys to know they're equal!

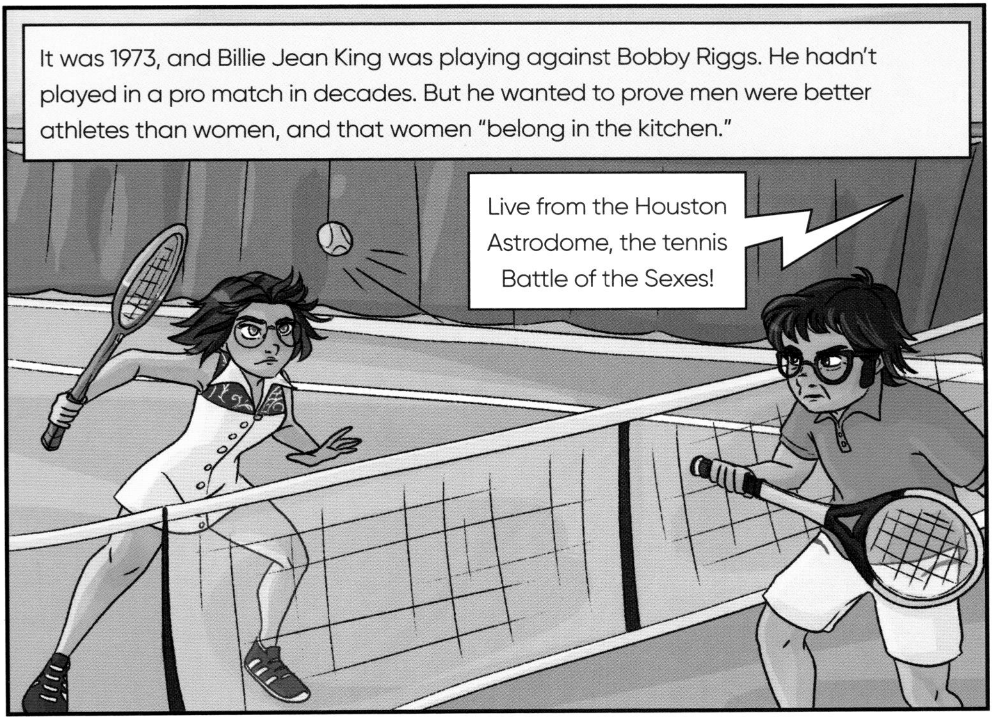
It was 1973, and Billie Jean King was playing against Bobby Riggs. He hadn't played in a pro match in decades. But he wanted to prove men were better athletes than women, and that women "belong in the kitchen."
Live from the Houston Astrodome, the tennis Battle of the Sexes!

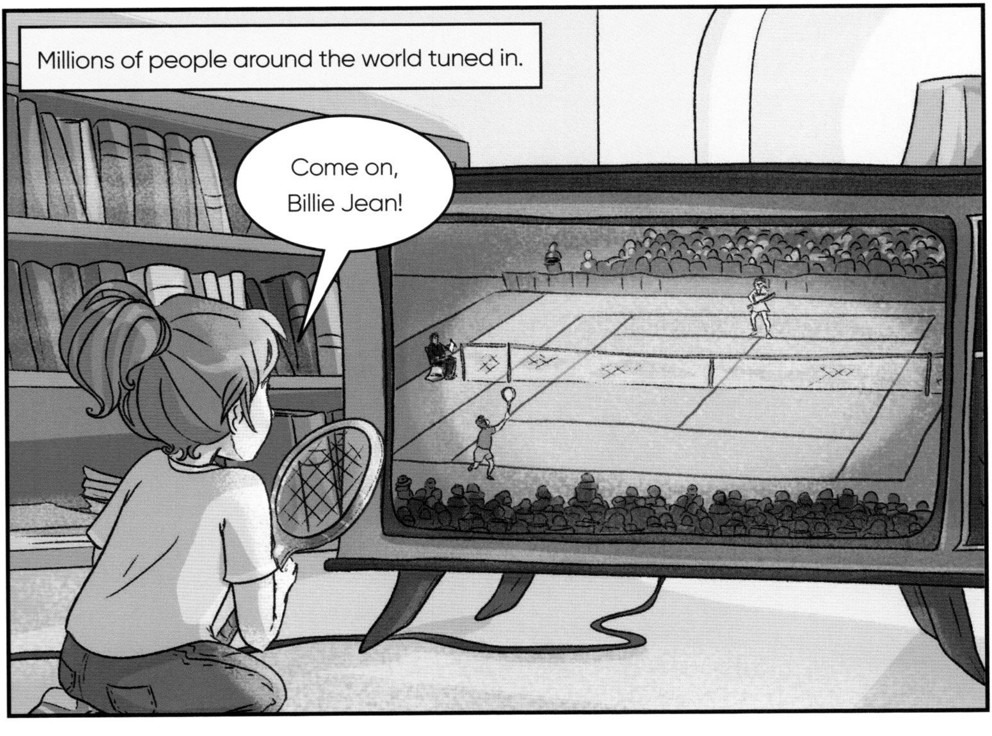
Millions of people around the world tuned in.
Come on, Billie Jean!

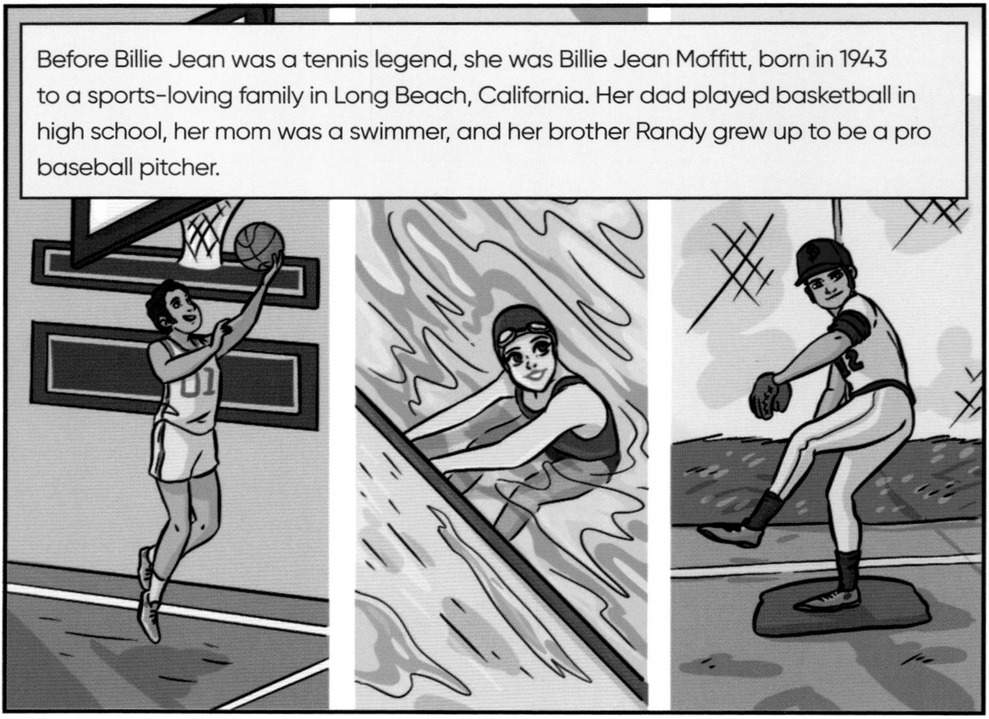
Before Billie Jean was a tennis legend, she was Billie Jean Moffitt, born in 1943 to a sports-loving family in Long Beach, California. Her dad played basketball in high school, her mom was a swimmer, and her brother Randy grew up to be a pro baseball pitcher.

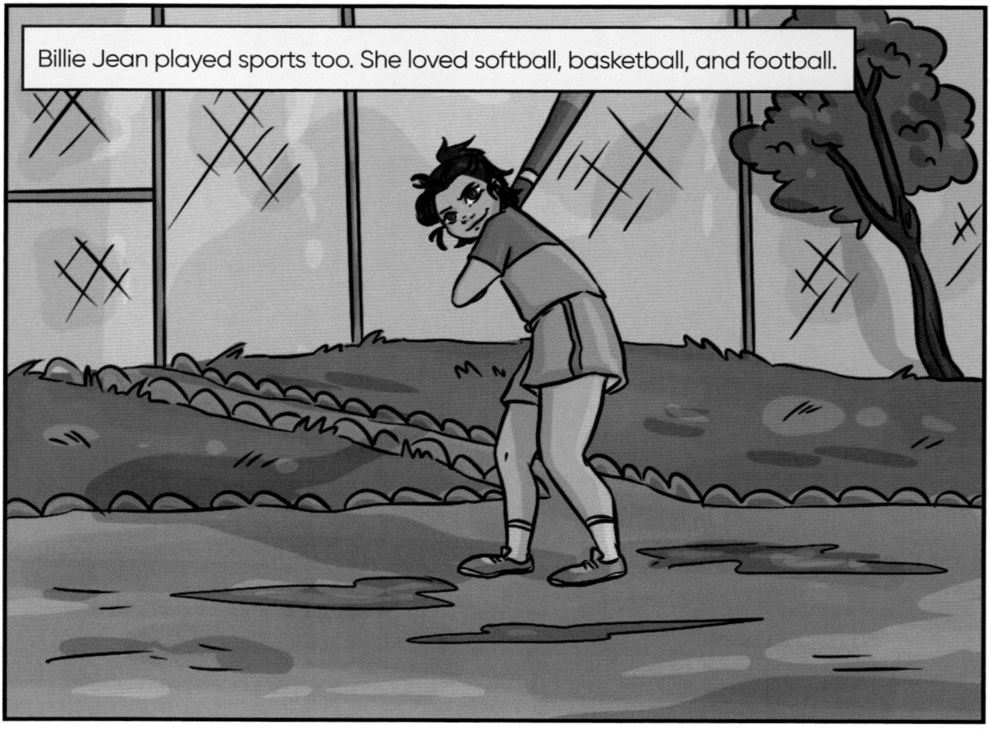
Billie Jean played sports too. She loved softball, basketball, and football.

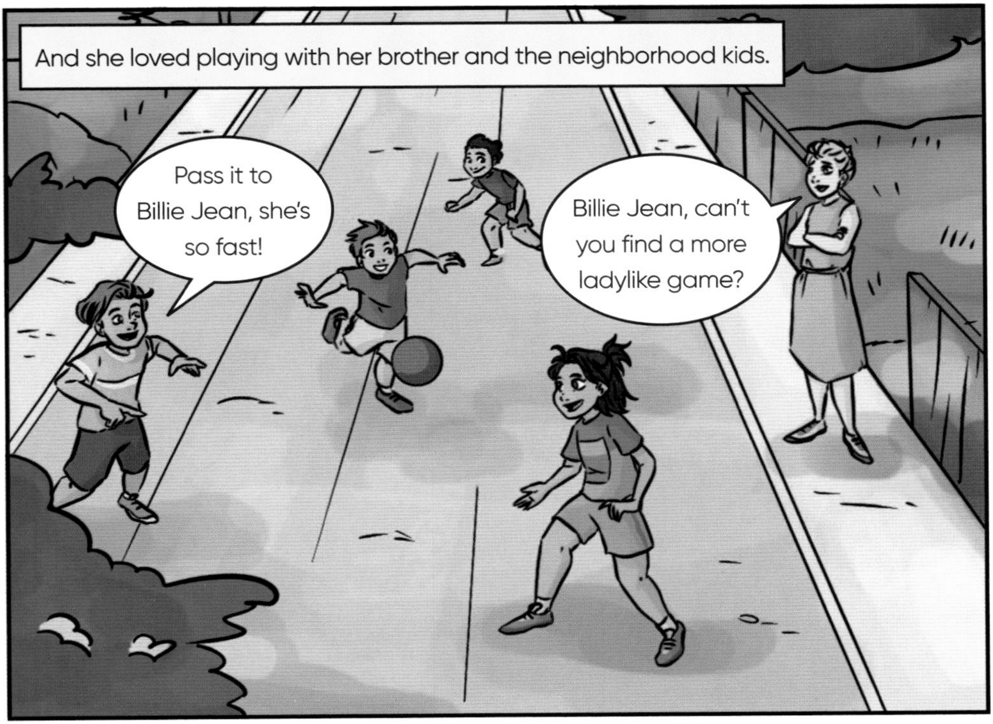
And she loved playing with her brother and the neighborhood kids.
Pass it to Billie Jean, she's so fast!
Billie Jean, can't you find a more ladylike game?

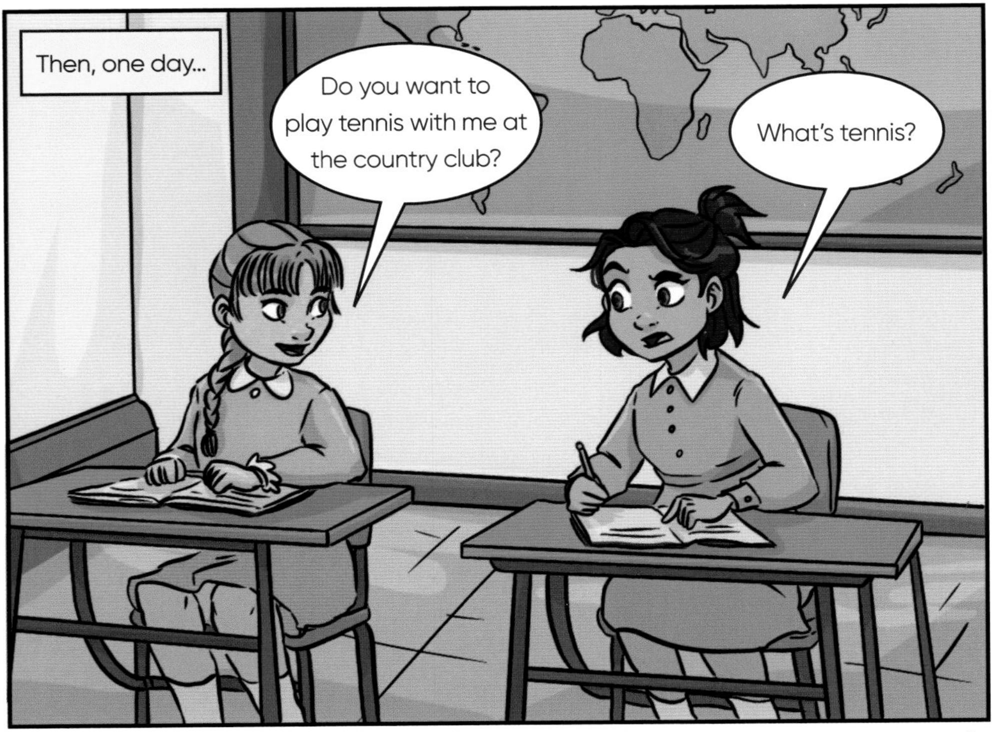
Then, one day...
Do you want to play tennis with me at the country club?
What's tennis?

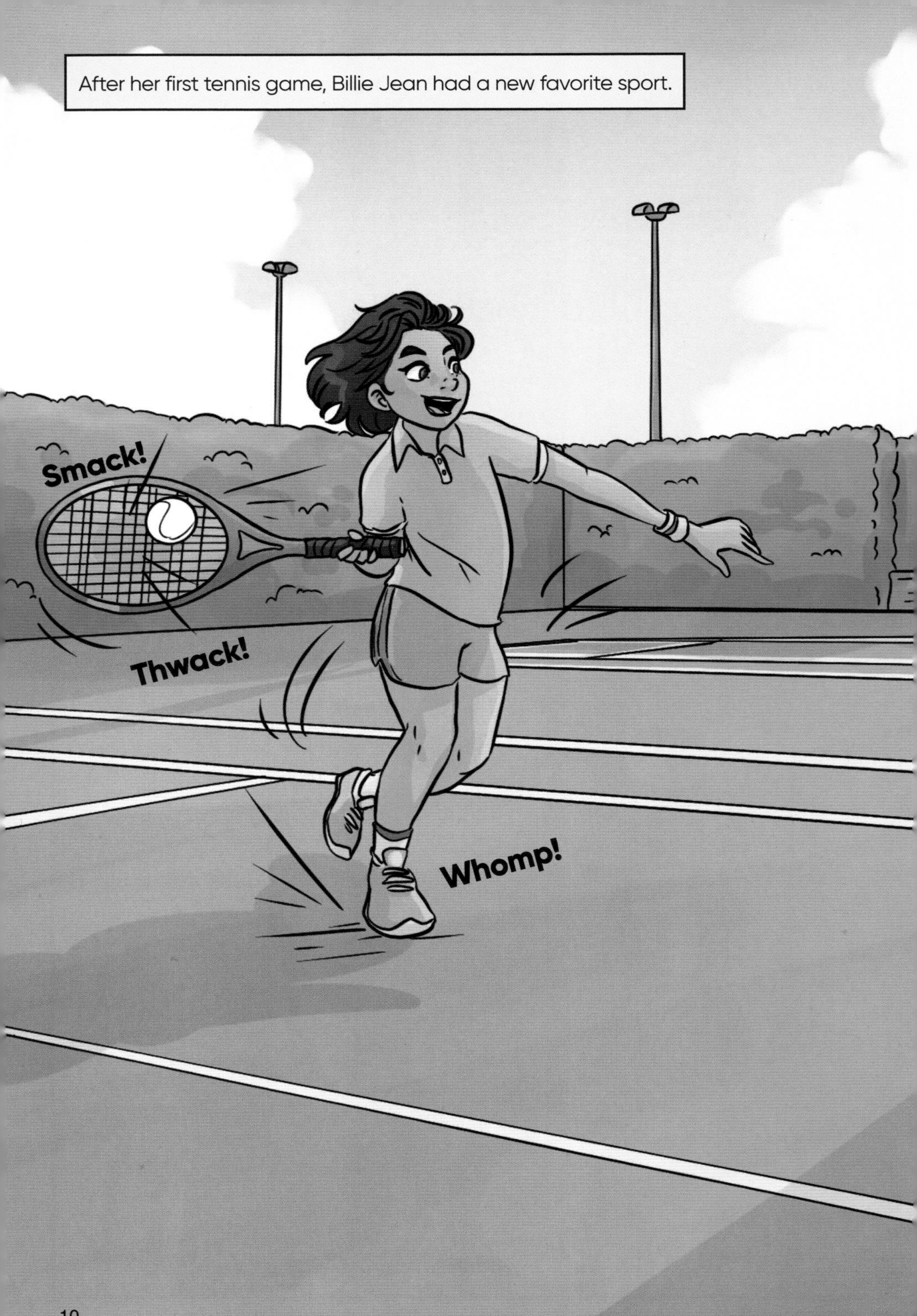
After her first tennis game, Billie Jean had a new favorite sport.
Smack!
Thwack!
Whomp!

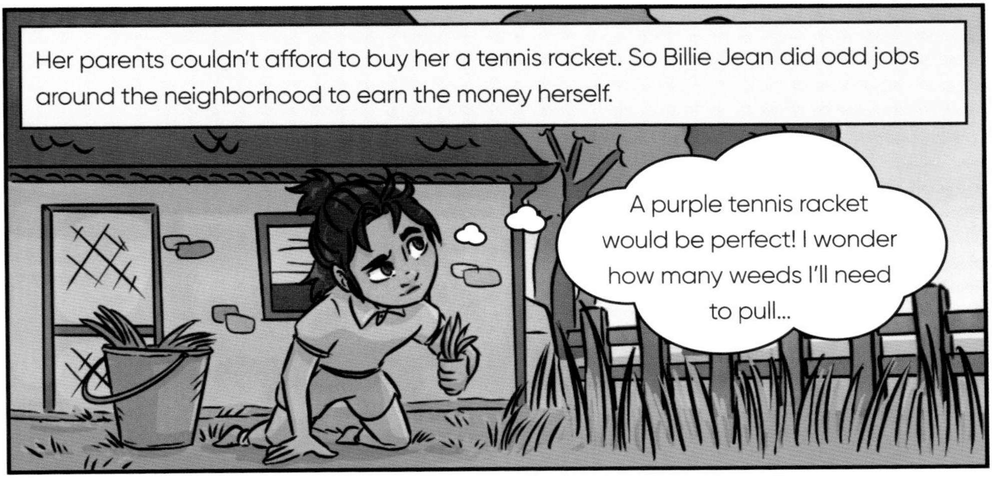
Her parents couldn't afford to buy her a tennis racket. So Billie Jean did odd jobs around the neighborhood to earn the money herself.
A purple tennis racket would be perfect! I wonder how many weeds I'll need to pull...

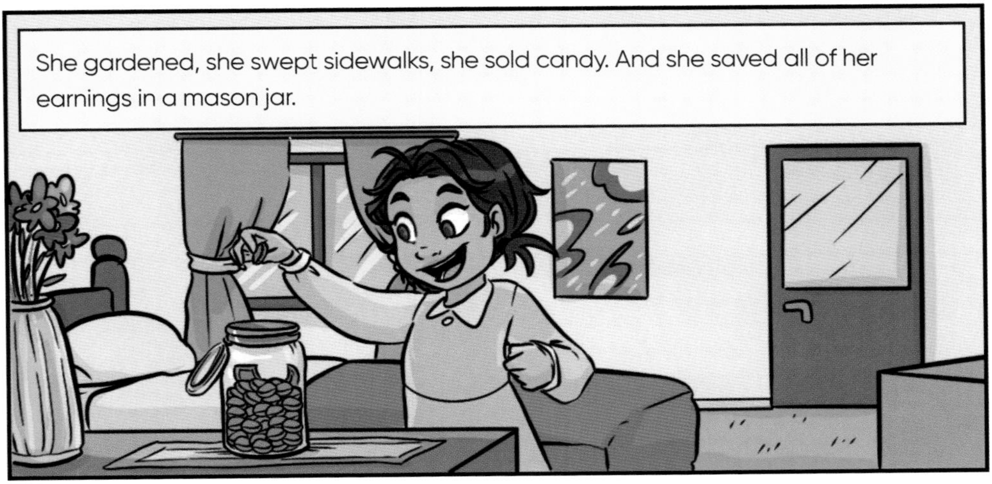
She gardened, she swept sidewalks, she sold candy. And she saved all of her earnings in a mason jar.

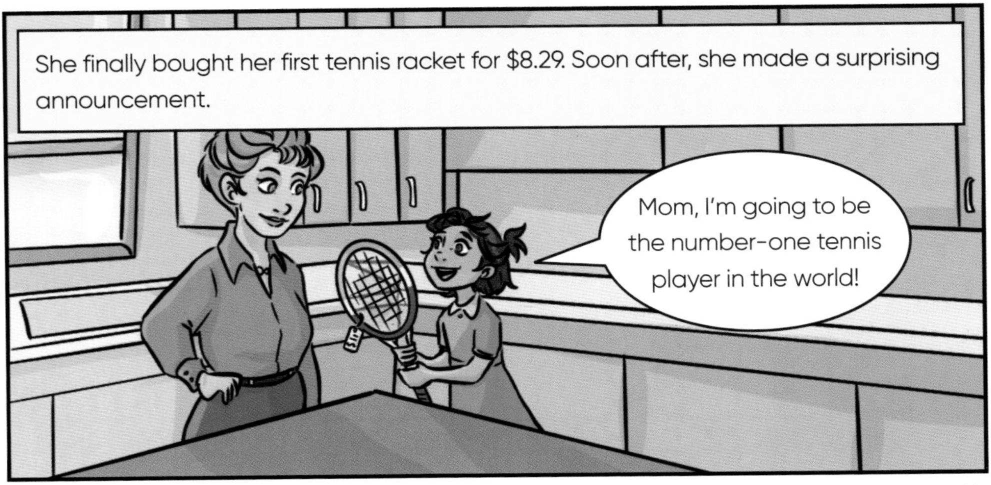
She finally bought her first tennis racket for $8.29. Soon after, she made a surprising announcement.
Mom, I'm going to be the number-one tennis player in the world!

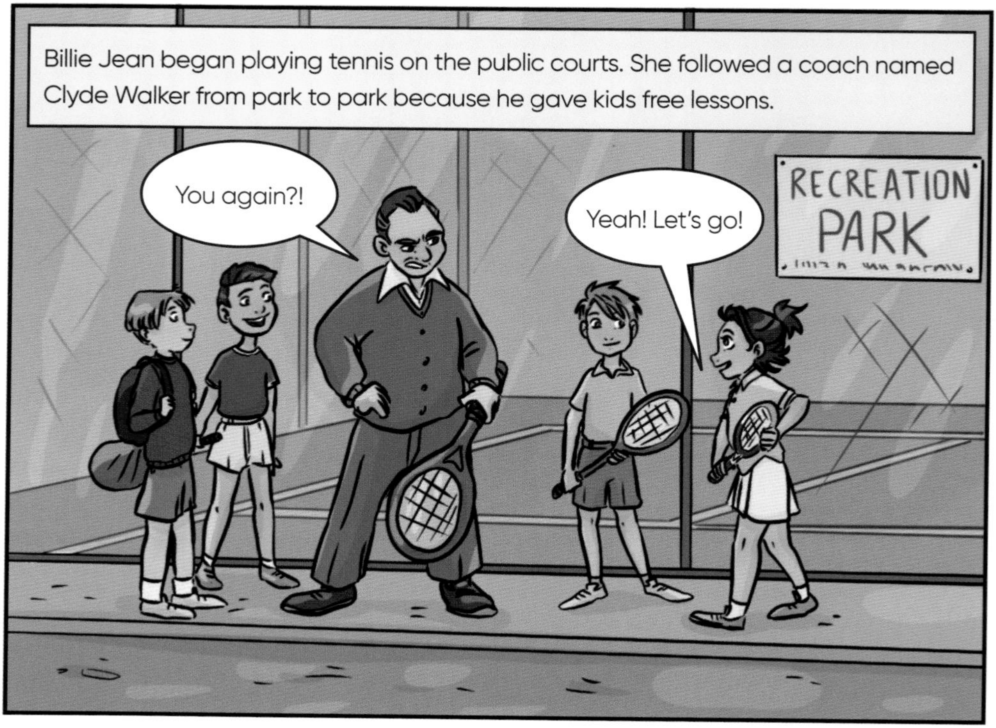
Billie Jean began playing tennis on the public courts. She followed a coach named Clyde Walker from park to park because he gave kids free lessons.
You again?!
Yeah! Let's go!
RECREATION PARK

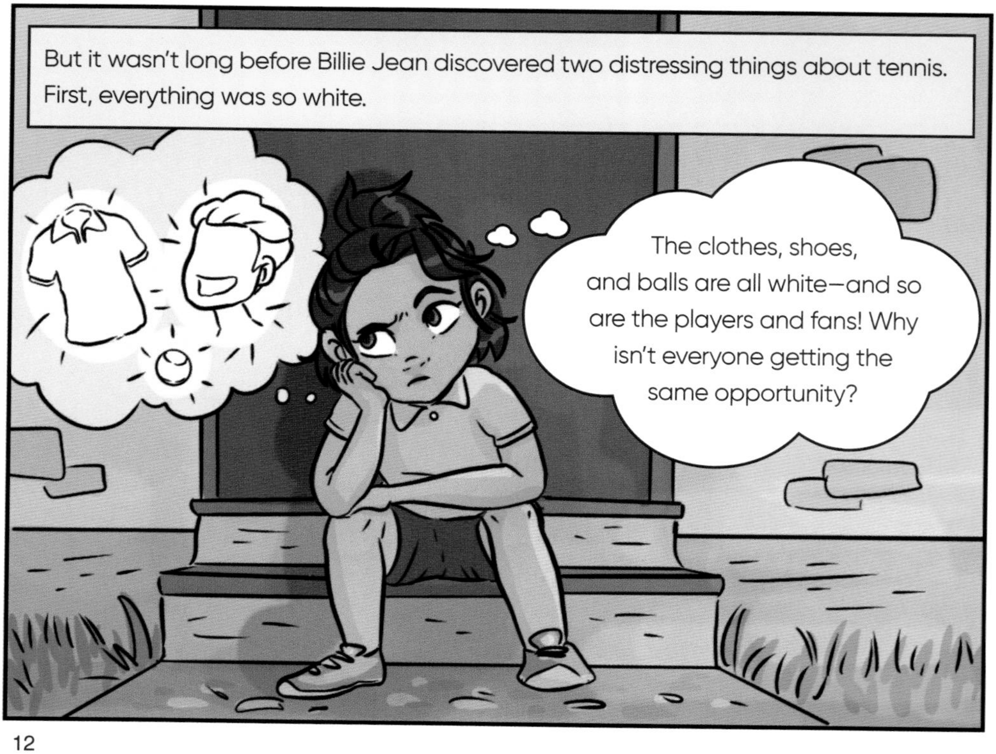
But it wasn't long before Billie Jean discovered two distressing things about tennis. First, everything was so white.
The clothes, shoes, and balls are all white—and so are the players and fans! Why isn't everyone getting the same opportunity?

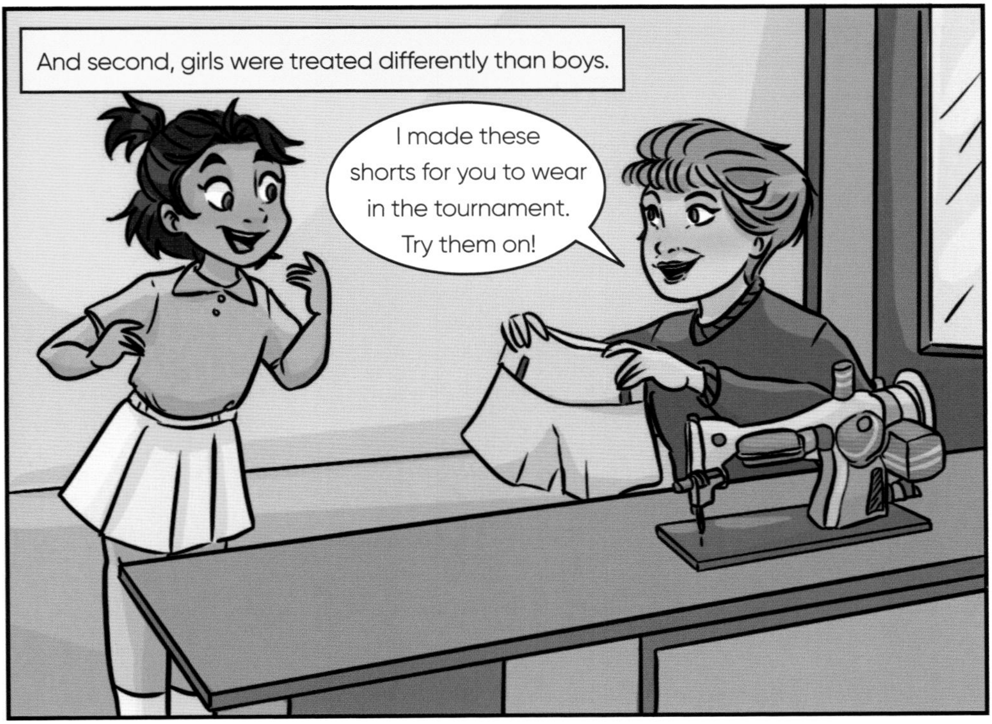
And second, girls were treated differently than boys.
I made these shorts for you to wear in the tournament. Try them on!

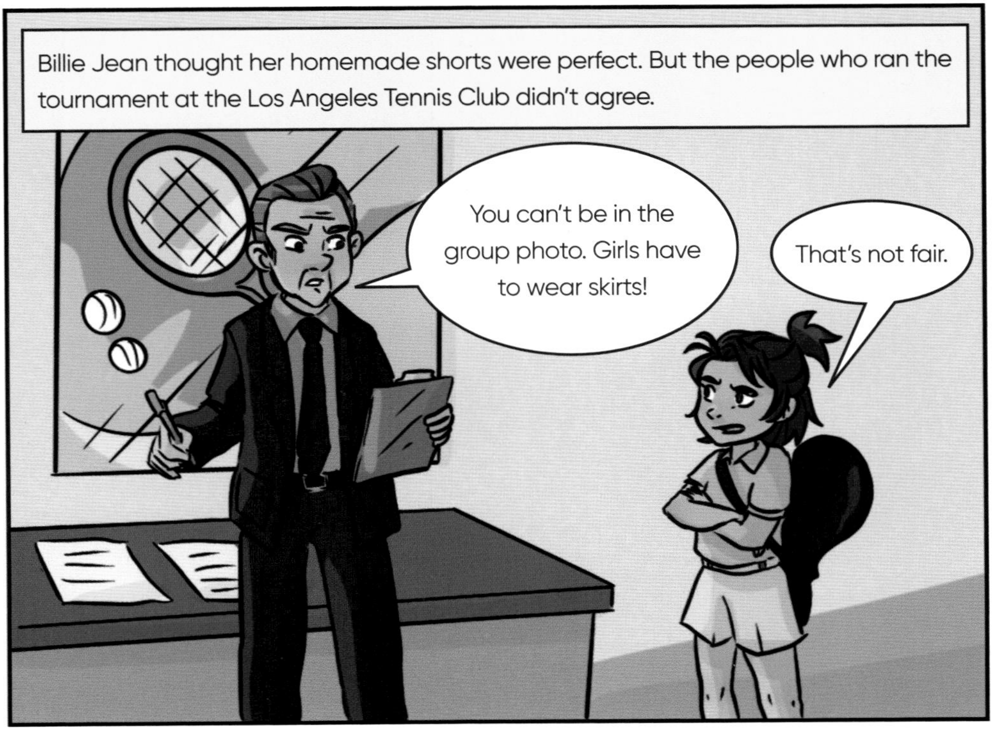
Billie Jean thought her homemade shorts were perfect. But the people who ran the tournament at the Los Angeles Tennis Club didn't agree.
You can't be in the group photo. Girls have to wear skirts!
That's not fair.

Being treated differently didn't stop Billie Jean. It just made her more determined to win. At seventeen, she won the Doubles Championship at Wimbledon with her partner Karen Hantze.

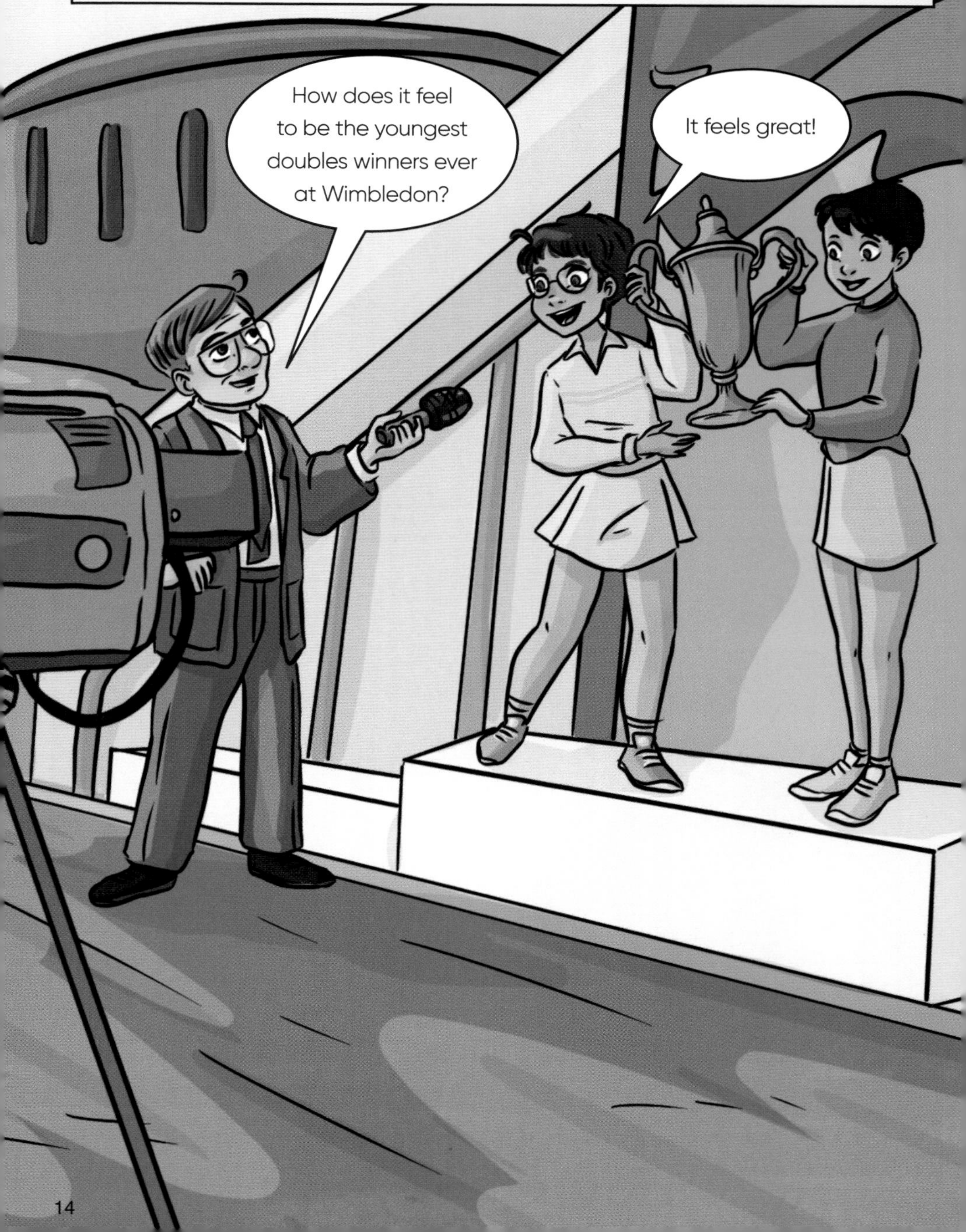
How does it feel to be the youngest doubles winners ever at Wimbledon?
It feels great!

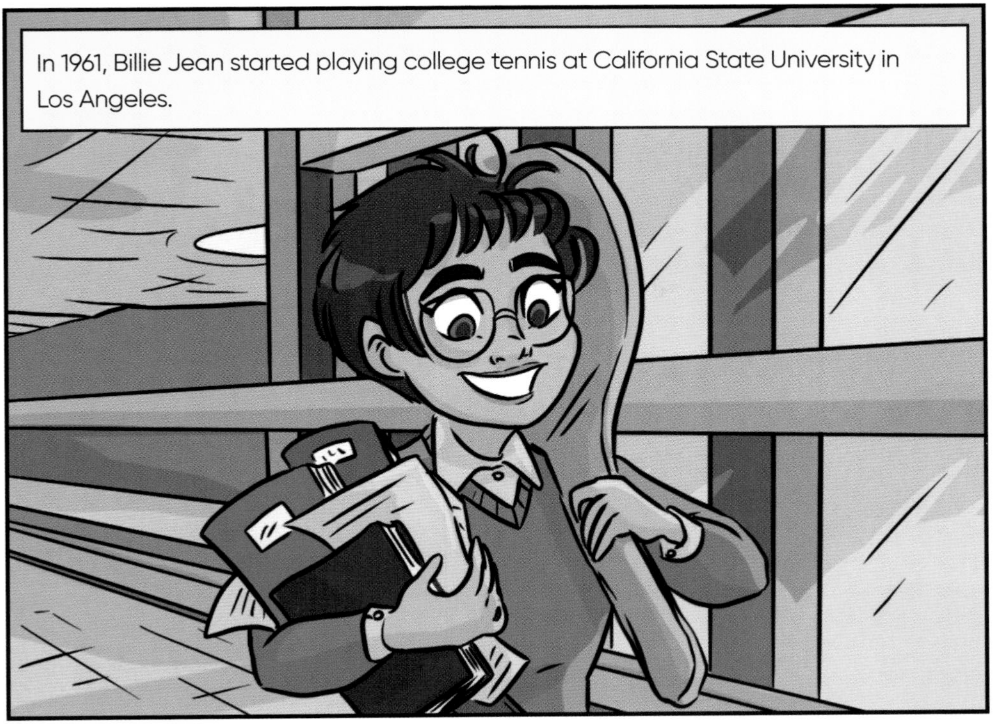
In 1961, Billie Jean started playing college tennis at California State University in Los Angeles.

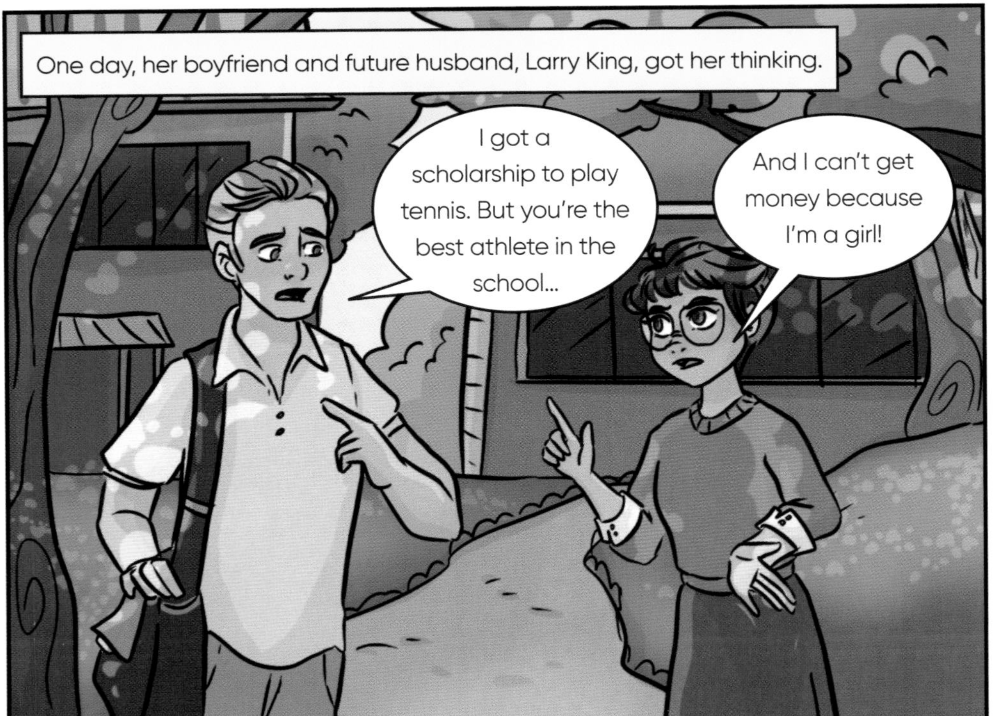
One day, her boyfriend and future husband, Larry King, got her thinking.
I got a scholarship to play tennis. But you're the best athlete in the school...
And I can't get money because I'm a girl!

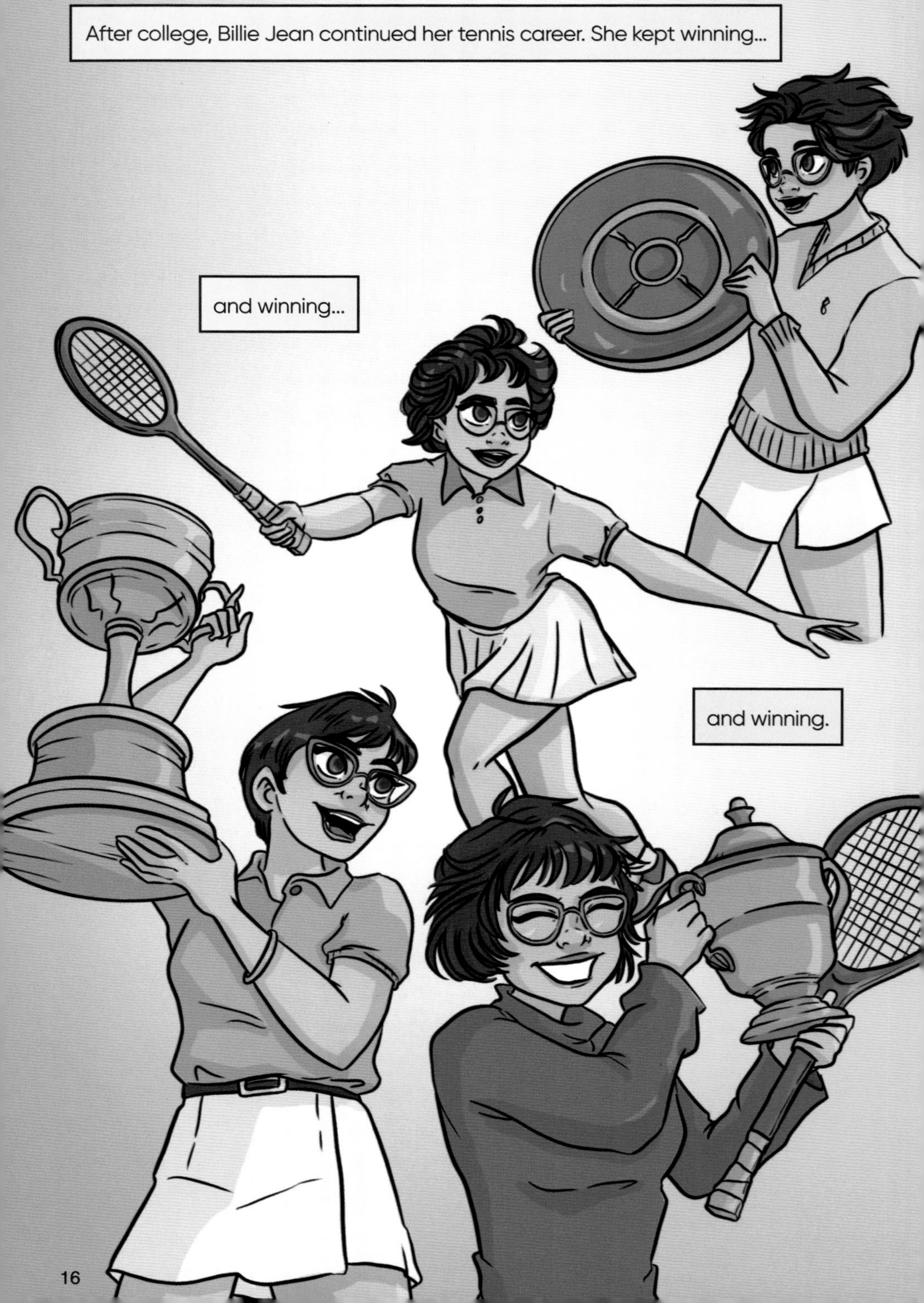
After college, Billie Jean continued her tennis career. She kept winning...
and winning...
and winning.

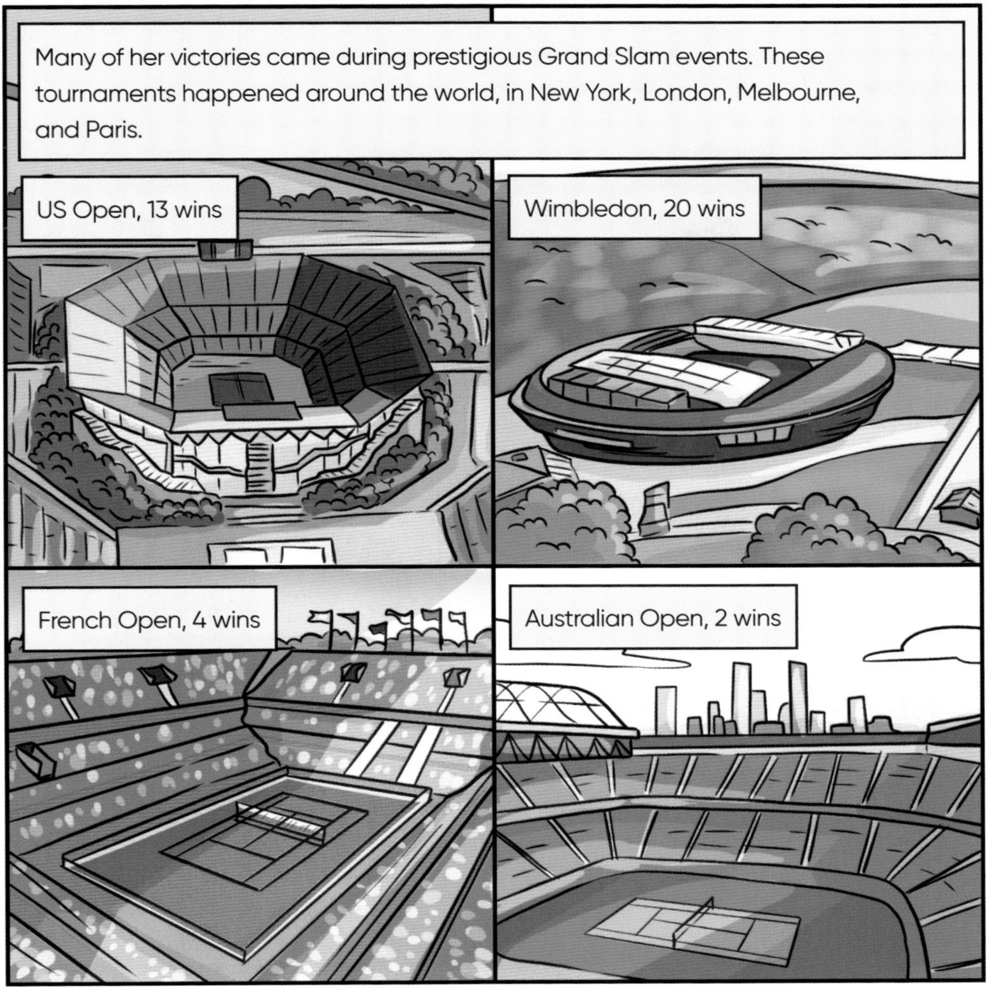
Many of her victories came during prestigious Grand Slam events. These tournaments happened around the world, in New York, London, Melbourne, and Paris.
US Open, 13 wins
Wimbledon, 20 wins
French Open, 4 wins
Australian Open, 2 wins

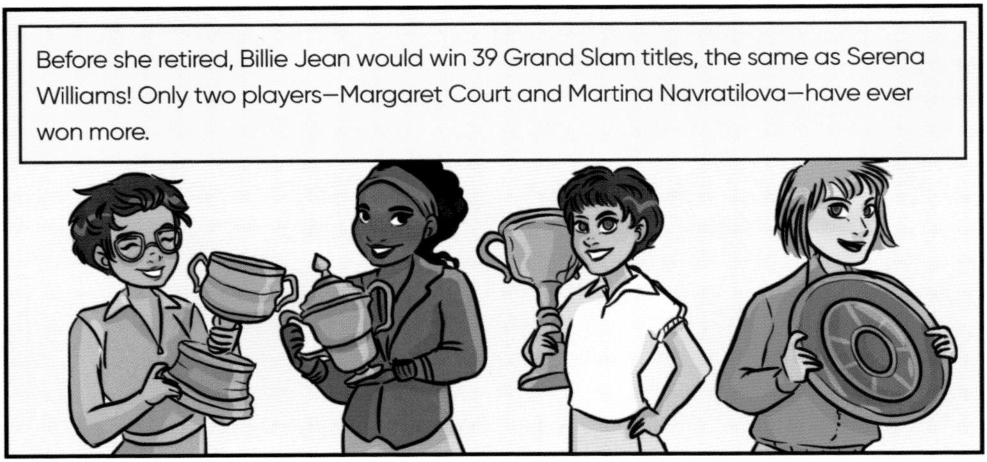
Before she retired, Billie Jean would win 39 Grand Slam titles, the same as Serena Williams! Only two players—Margaret Court and Martina Navratilova—have ever won more.

By 1966, Billie Jean—now Billie Jean King—was the number-one female tennis player in the world!

Just like I told my mom!

Billie Jean was number one again in 1967...

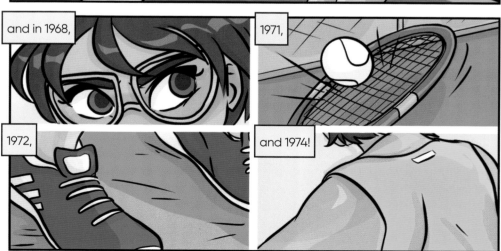

and in 1968,

1971,

1972,

and 1974!

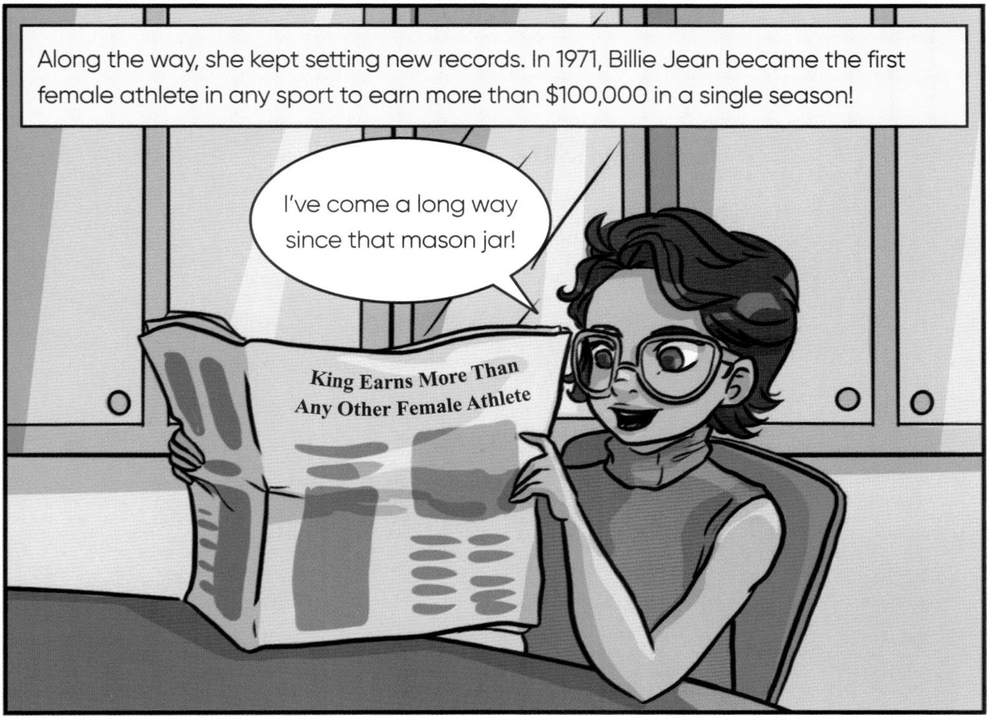
Along the way, she kept setting new records. In 1971, Billie Jean became the first female athlete in any sport to earn more than $100,000 in a single season!
I've come a long way since that mason jar!
King Earns More Than Any Other Female Athlete

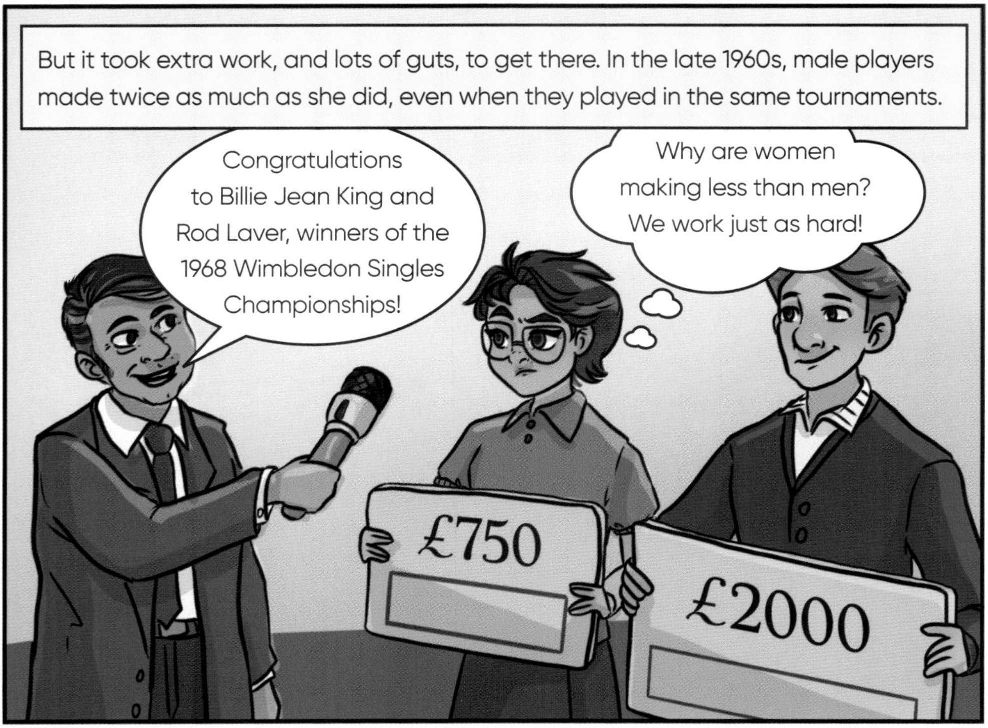
But it took extra work, and lots of guts, to get there. In the late 1960s, male players made twice as much as she did, even when they played in the same tournaments.
Congratulations to Billie Jean King and Rod Laver, winners of the 1968 Wimbledon Singles Championships!
Why are women making less than men? We work just as hard!
£750
£2000

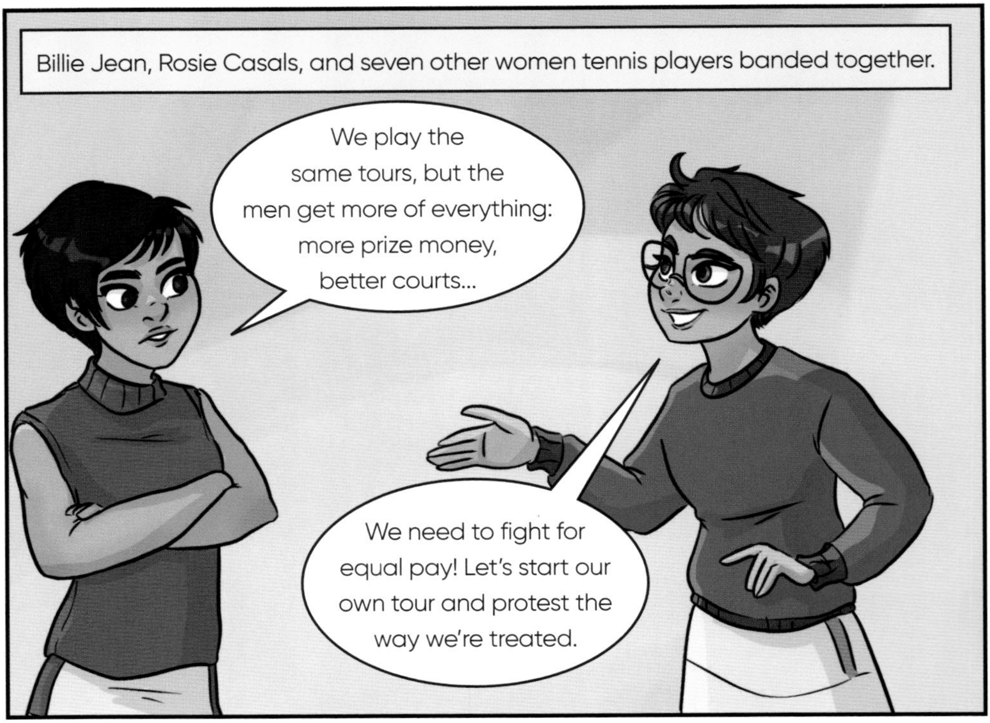
Billie Jean, Rosie Casals, and seven other women tennis players banded together.
We play the same tours, but the men get more of everything: more prize money, better courts...
We need to fight for equal pay! Let's start our own tour and protest the way we're treated.

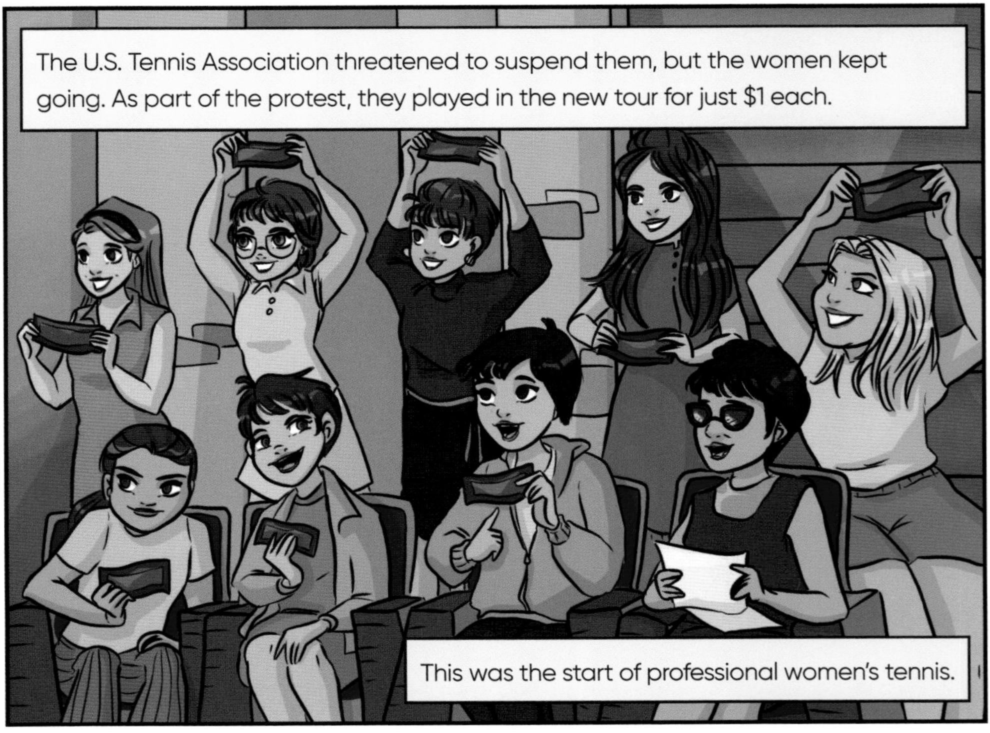
The U.S. Tennis Association threatened to suspend them, but the women kept going. As part of the protest, they played in the new tour for just $1 each.
This was the start of professional women's tennis.

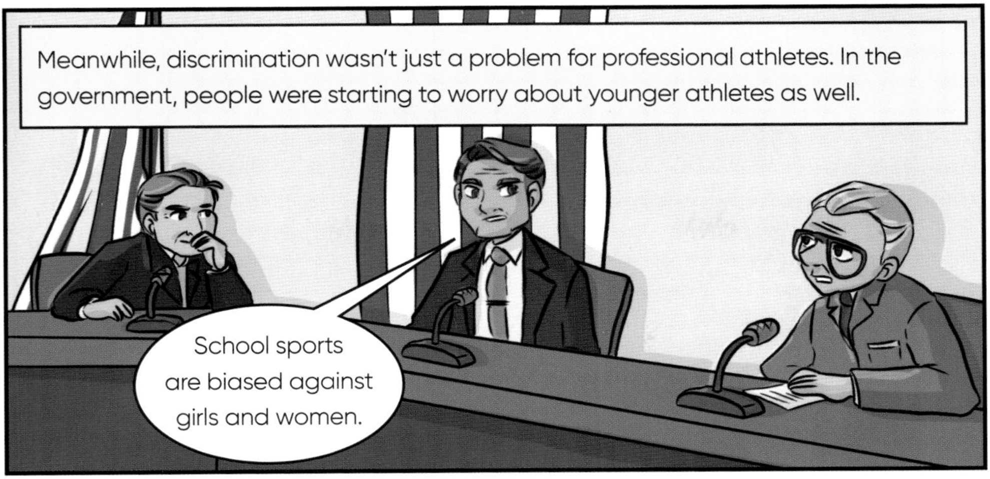
Meanwhile, discrimination wasn't just a problem for professional athletes. In the government, people were starting to worry about younger athletes as well.
School sports are biased against girls and women.

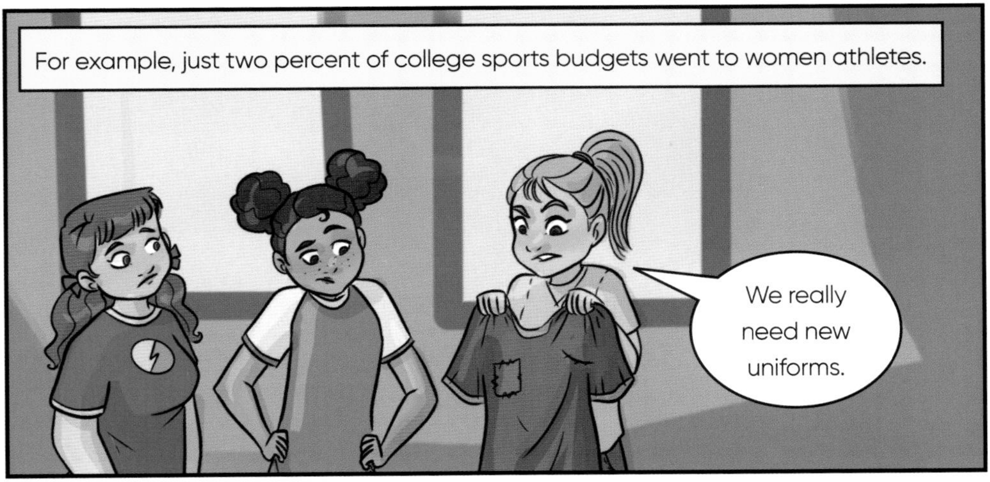
For example, just two percent of college sports budgets went to women athletes.
We really need new uniforms.

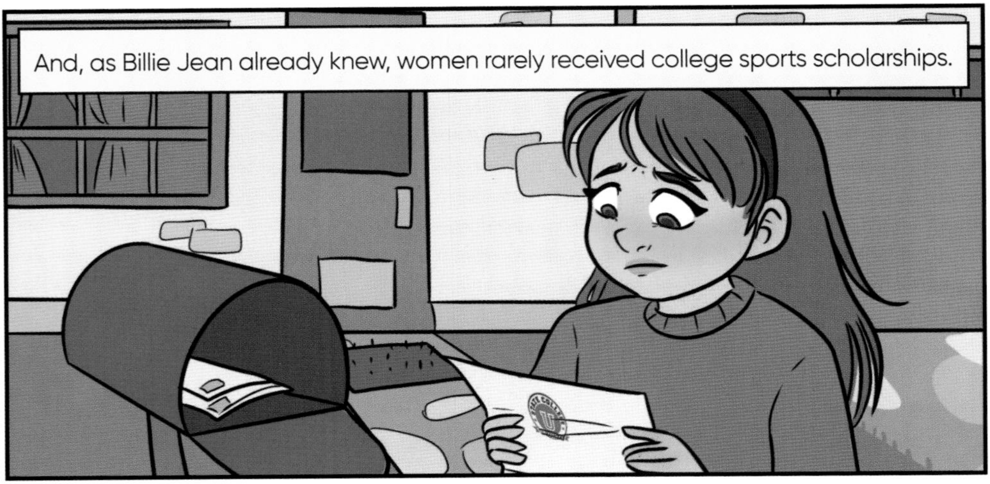
And, as Billie Jean already knew, women rarely received college sports scholarships.

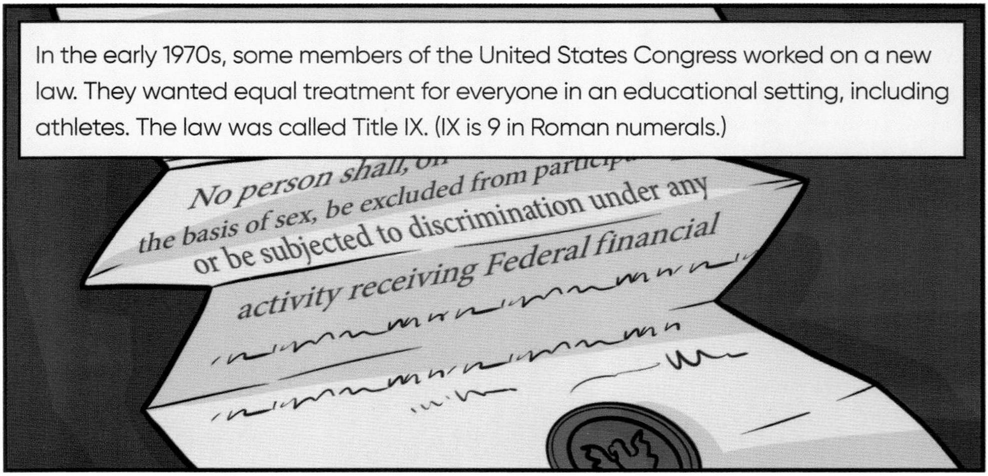
In the early 1970s, some members of the United States Congress worked on a new law. They wanted equal treatment for everyone in an educational setting, including athletes. The law was called Title IX. (IX is 9 in Roman numerals.)
No person shall,
the basis of sex, be excluded from
or be subjected to discrimination under any
activity receiving Federal financial

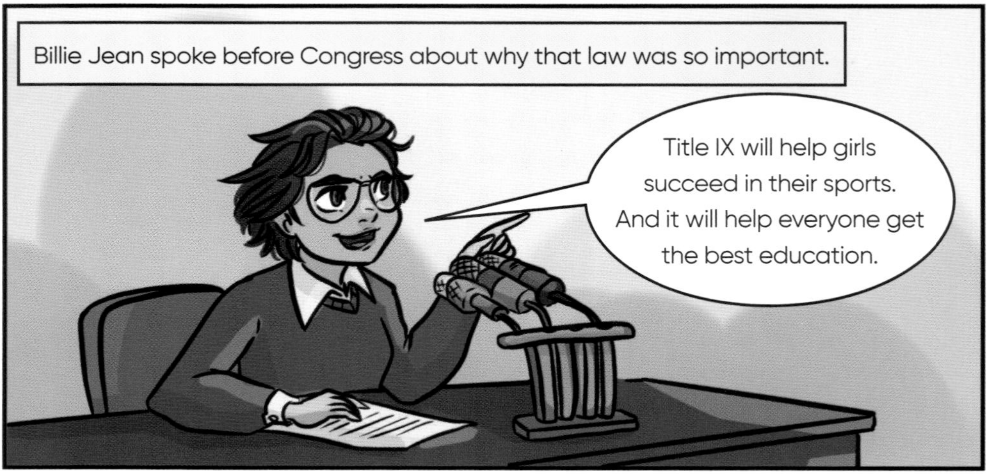
Billie Jean spoke before Congress about why that law was so important.
Title IX will help girls succeed in their sports. And it will help everyone get the best education.

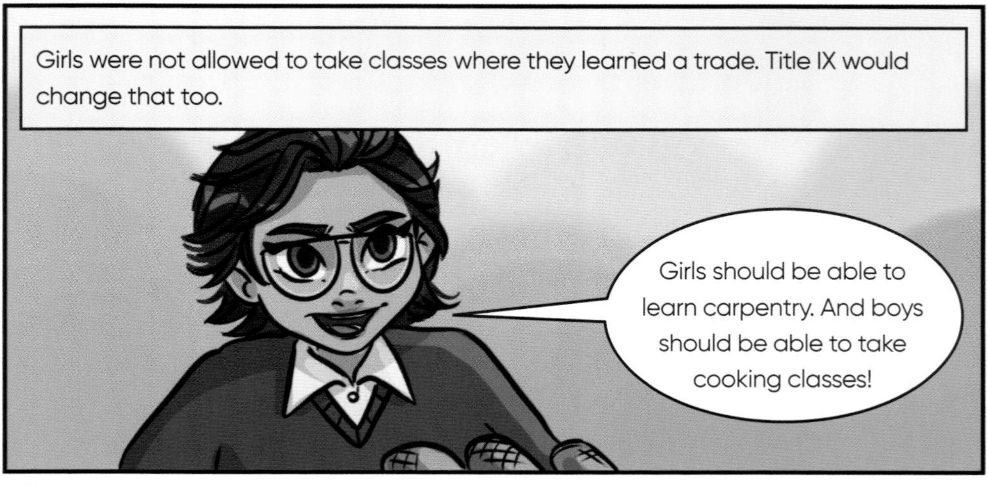
Girls were not allowed to take classes where they learned a trade. Title IX would change that too.
Girls should be able to learn carpentry. And boys should be able to take cooking classes!

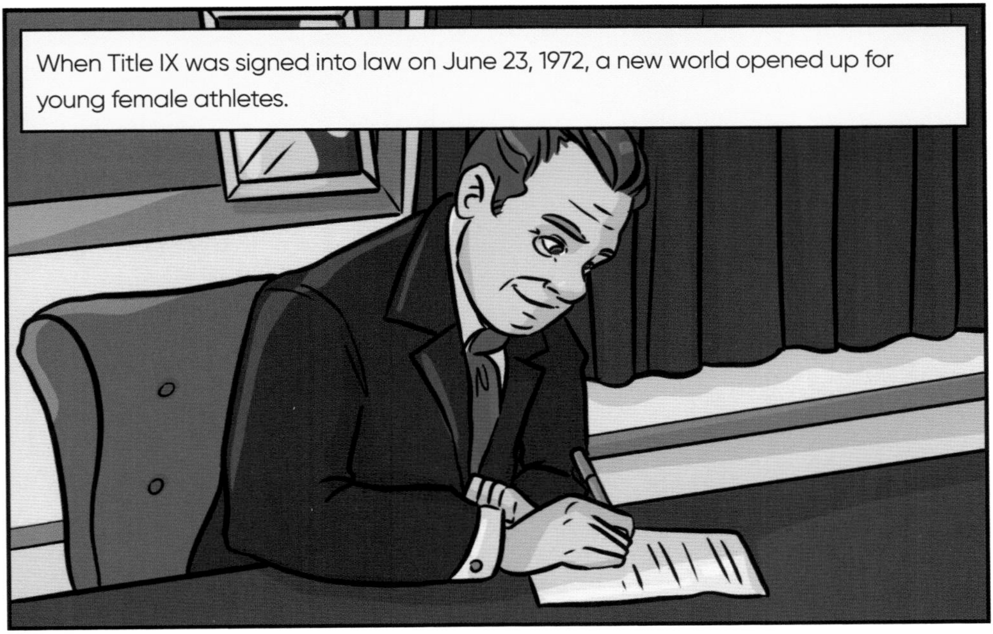
When Title IX was signed into law on June 23, 1972, a new world opened up for young female athletes.

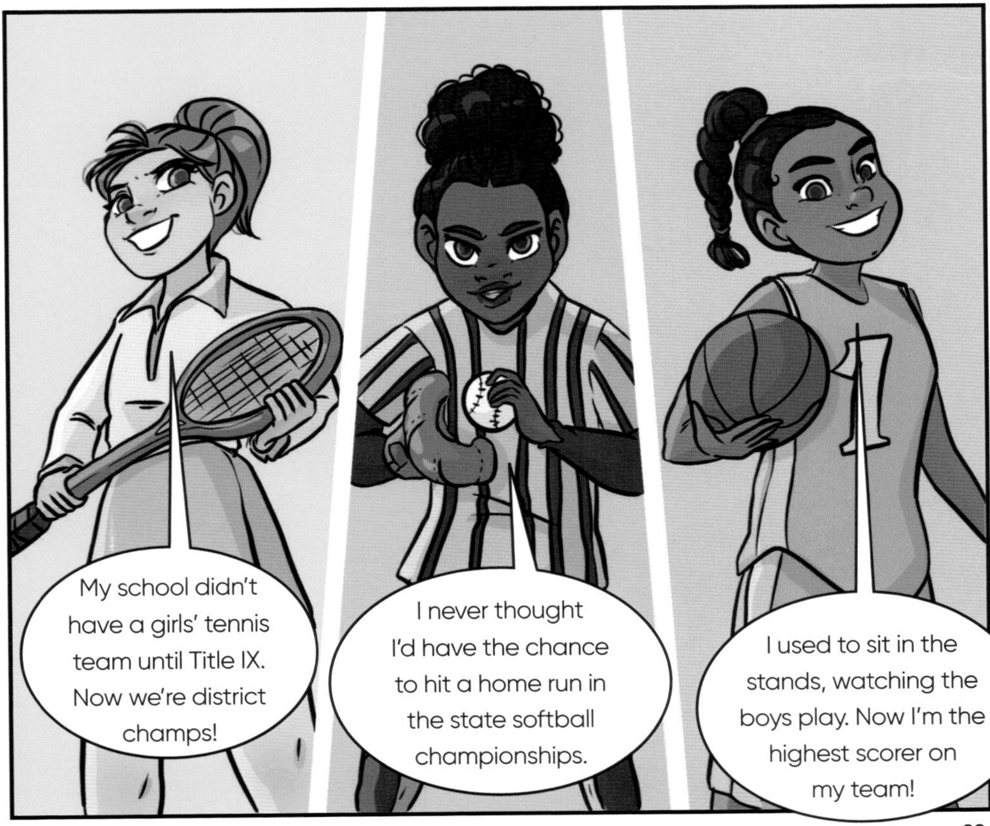
My school didn't have a girls' tennis team until Title IX. Now we're district champs!
I never thought I'd have the chance to hit a home run in the state softball championships.
I used to sit in the stands, watching the boys play. Now I'm the highest scorer on my team!

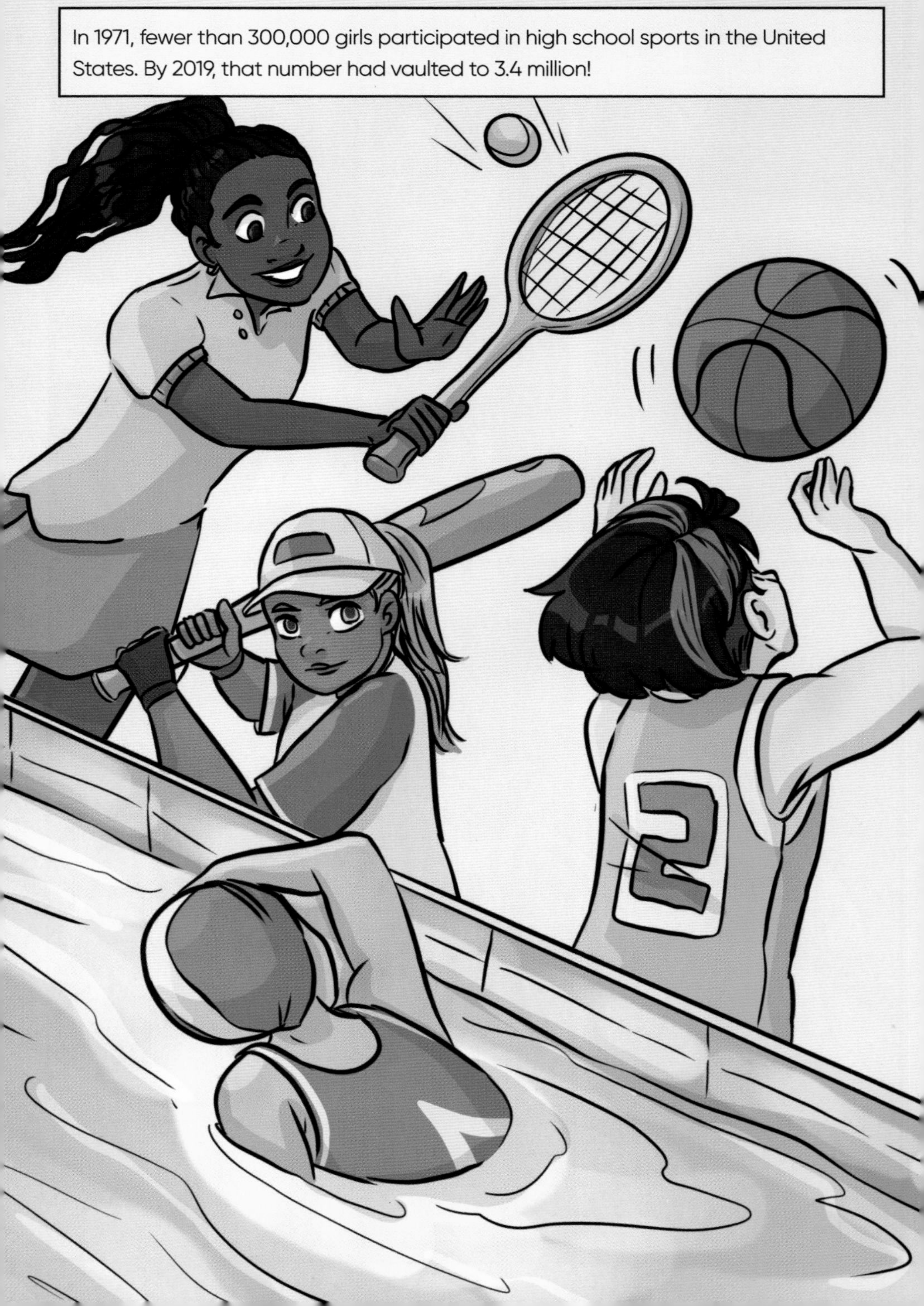
In 1971, fewer than 300,000 girls participated in high school sports in the United States. By 2019, that number had vaulted to 3.4 million!
2

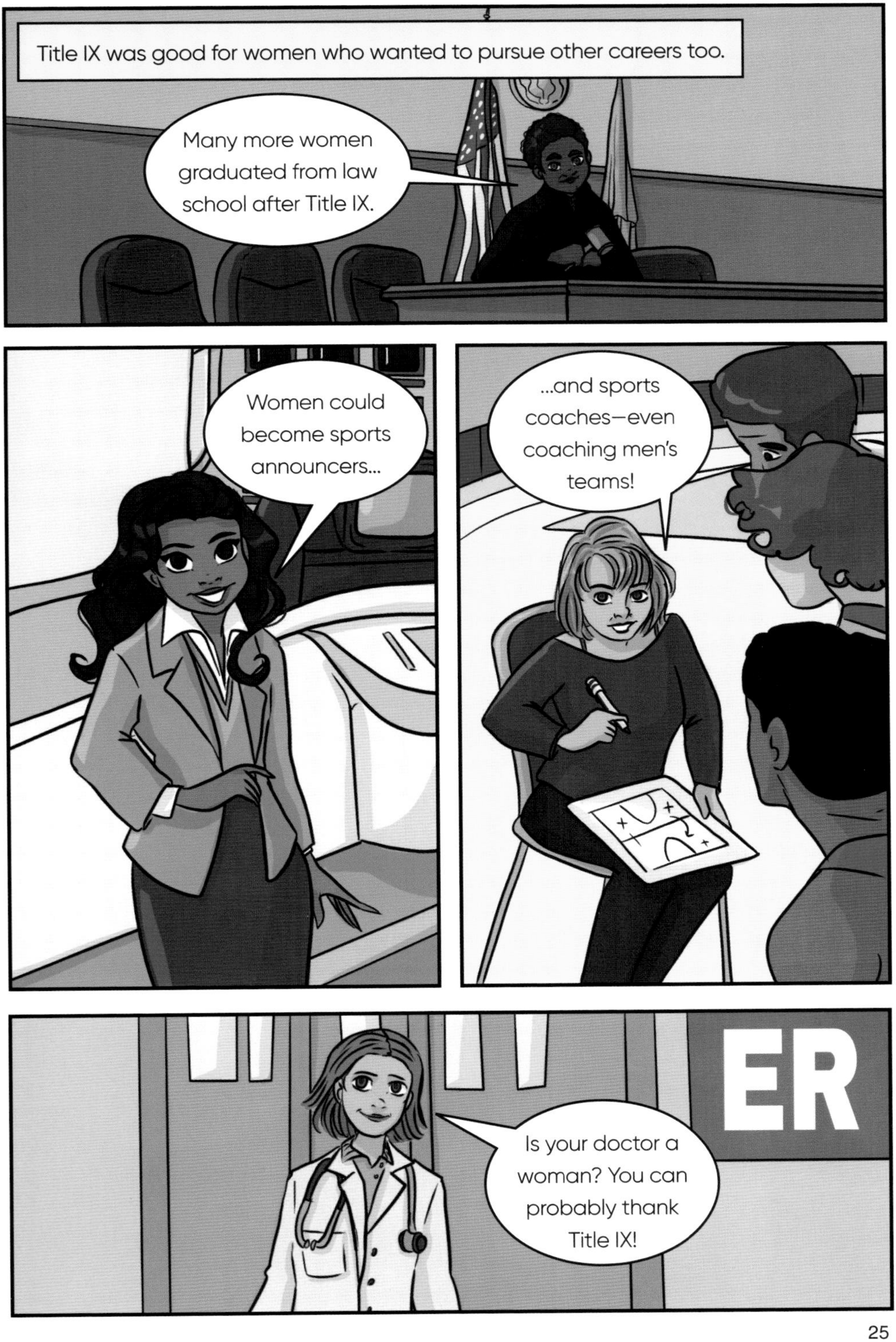
Title IX was good for women who wanted to pursue other careers too.
Many more women graduated from law school after Title IX.
Women could become sports announcers...
...and sports coaches—even coaching men's teams!
ER
Is your doctor a woman? You can probably thank Title IX!

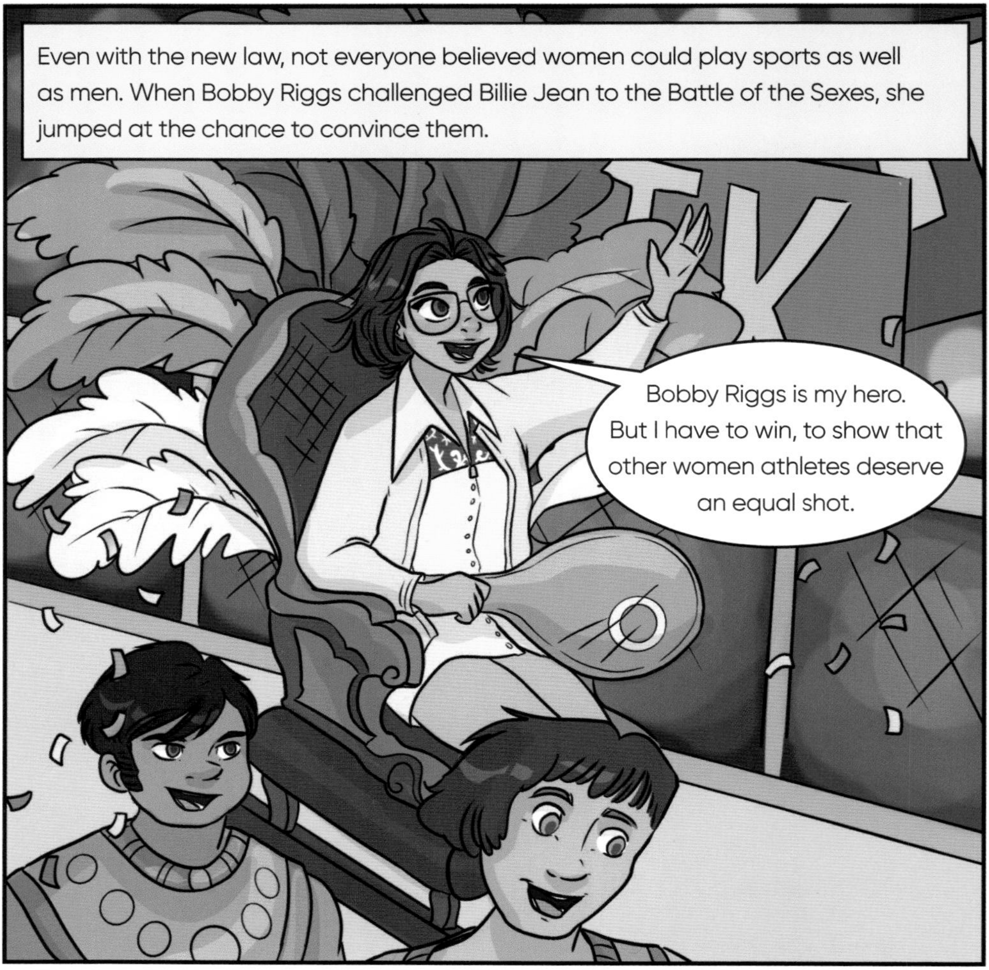
Even with the new law, not everyone believed women could play sports as well as men. When Bobby Riggs challenged Billie Jean to the Battle of the Sexes, she jumped at the chance to convince them.
Bobby Riggs is my hero. But I have to win, to show that other women athletes deserve an equal shot.

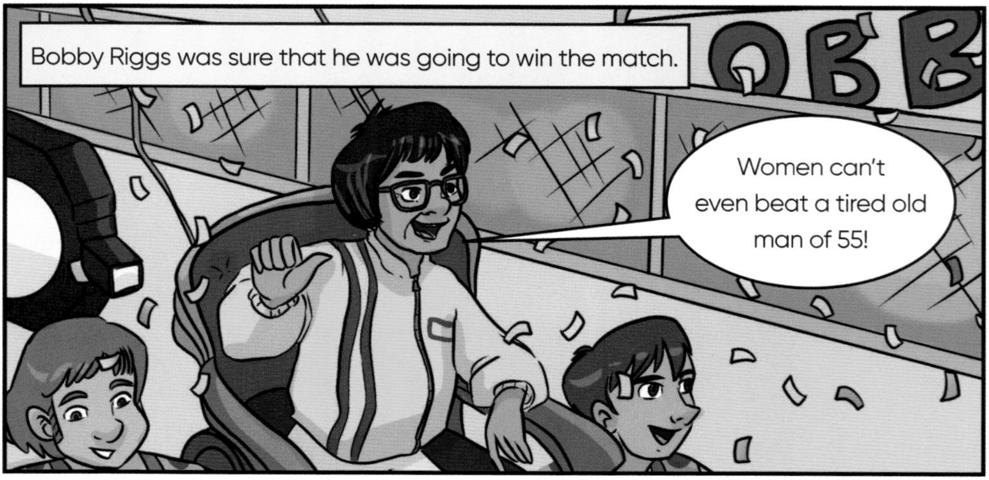
Bobby Riggs was sure that he was going to win the match.
OBB
Women can't even beat a tired old man of 55!

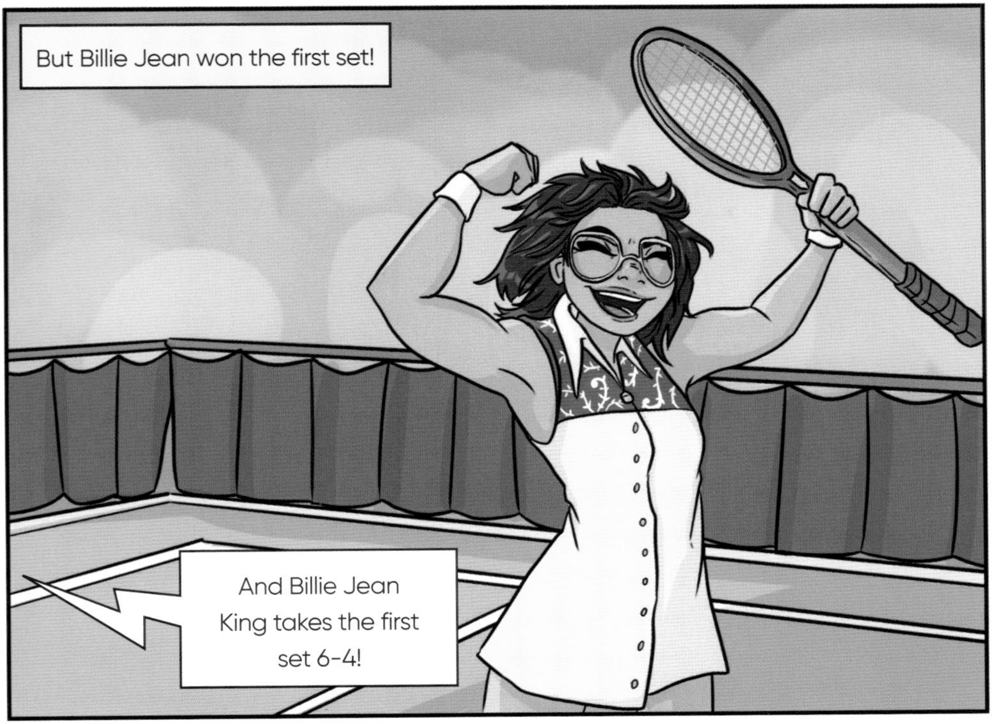
But Billie Jean won the first set!
And Billie Jean King takes the first set 6-4!

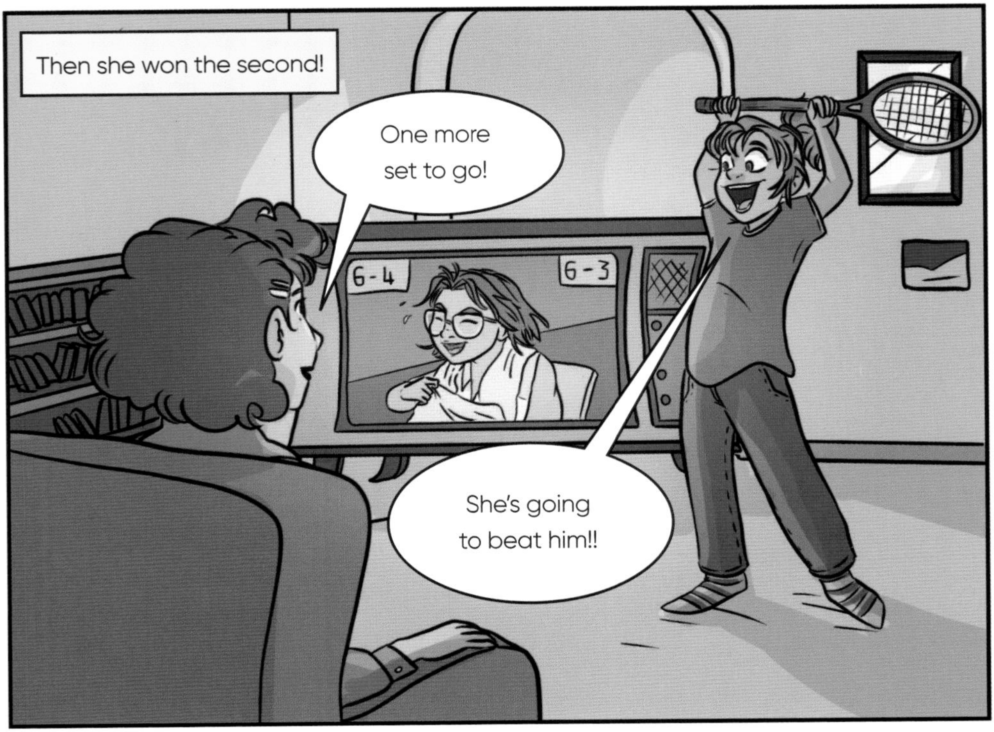
Then she won the second!
One more set to go!
6-4
6-3
She's going to beat him!!

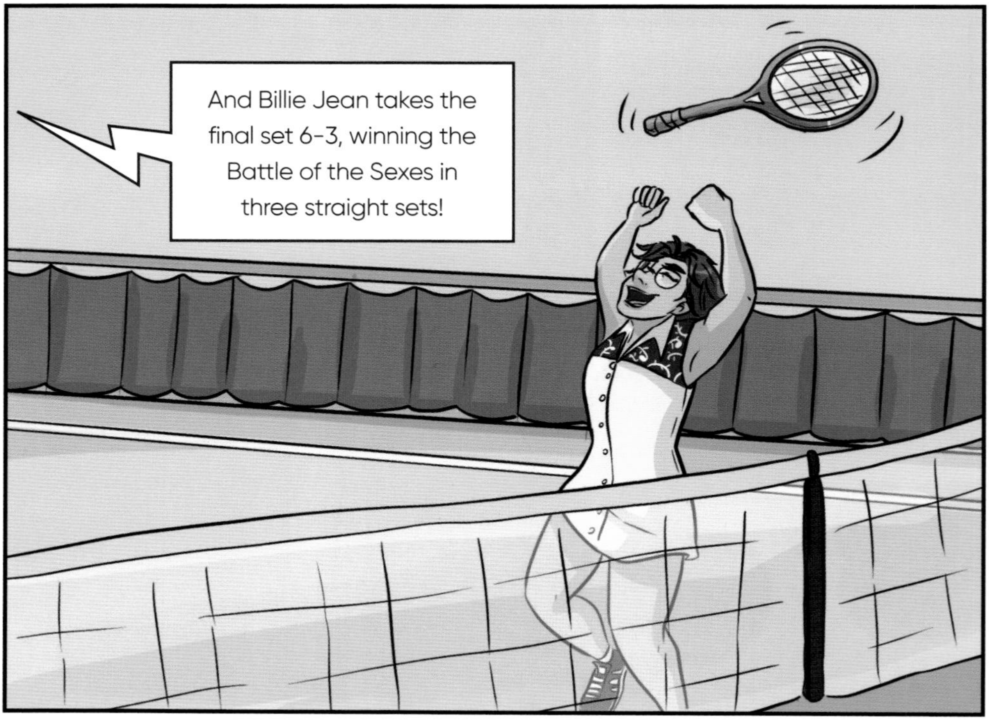
And Billie Jean takes the final set 6-3, winning the Battle of the Sexes in three straight sets!

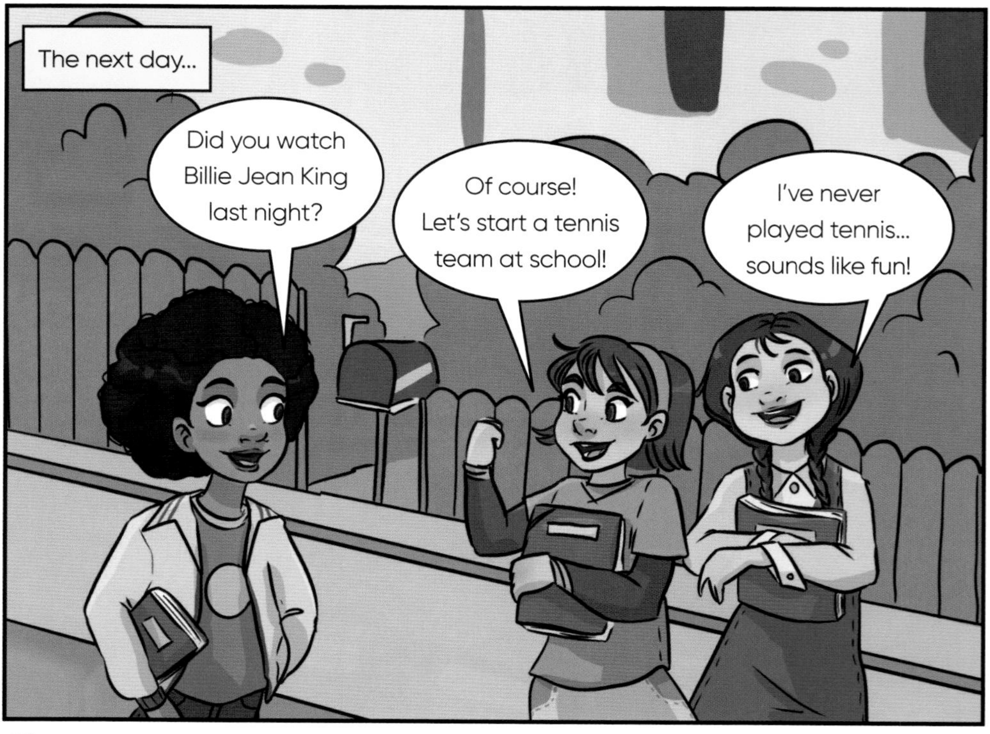
The next day...
Did you watch Billie Jean King last night?
Of course! Let's start a tennis team at school!
I've never played tennis... sounds like fun!

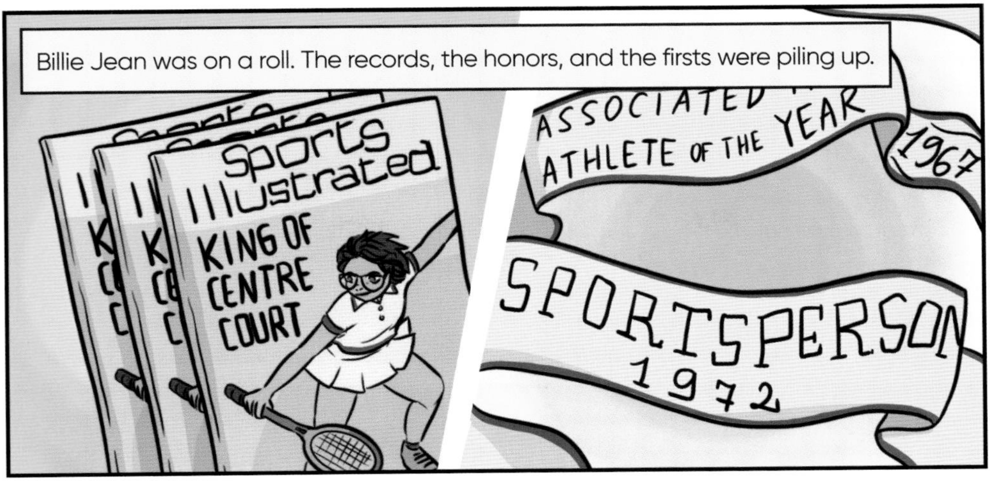
Billie Jean was on a roll. The records, the honors, and the firsts were piling up.
Sports Illustrated
KING OF CENTRE COURT
ASSOCIATED
ATHLETE OF THE YEAR
1967
SPORTSPERSON
1972

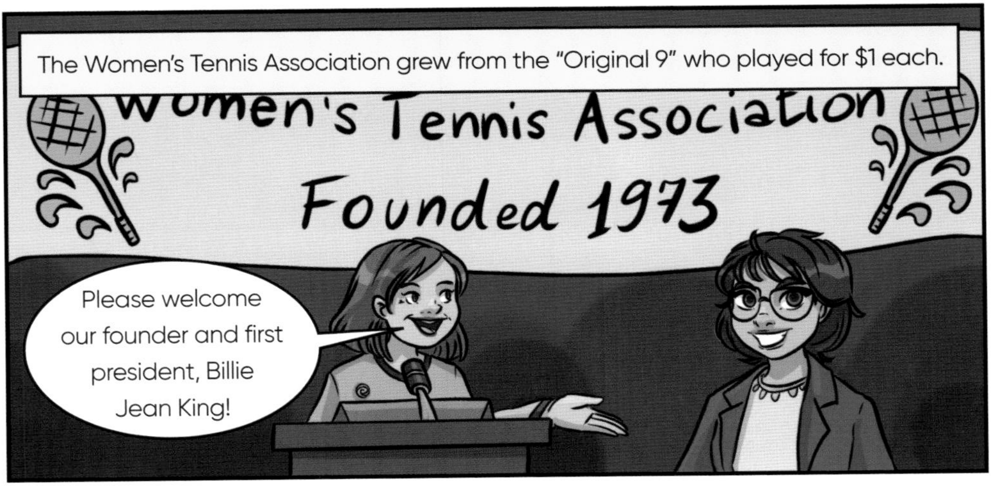
The Women's Tennis Association grew from the "Original 9" who played for $1 each.
Women's Tennis Association
Founded 1973
Please welcome our founder and first president, Billie Jean King!

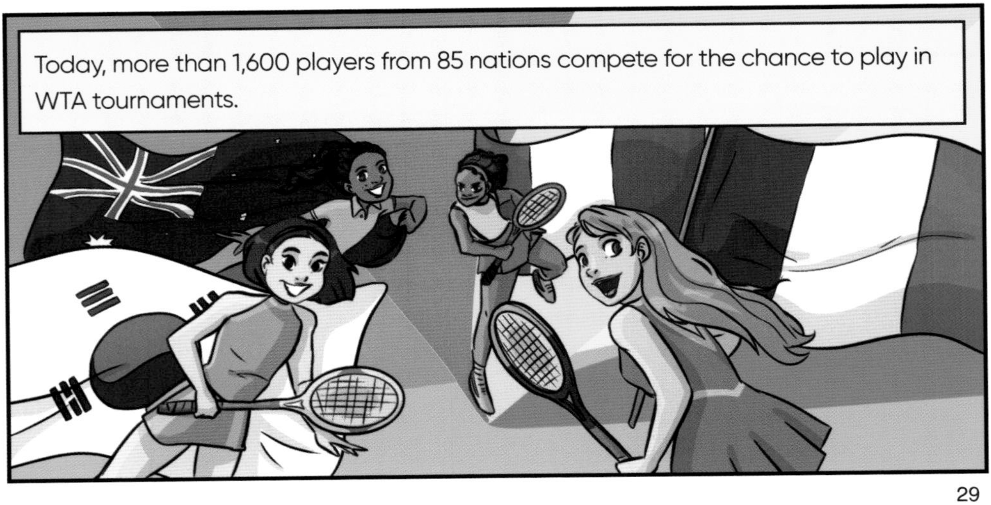
Today, more than 1,600 players from 85 nations compete for the chance to play in WTA tournaments.

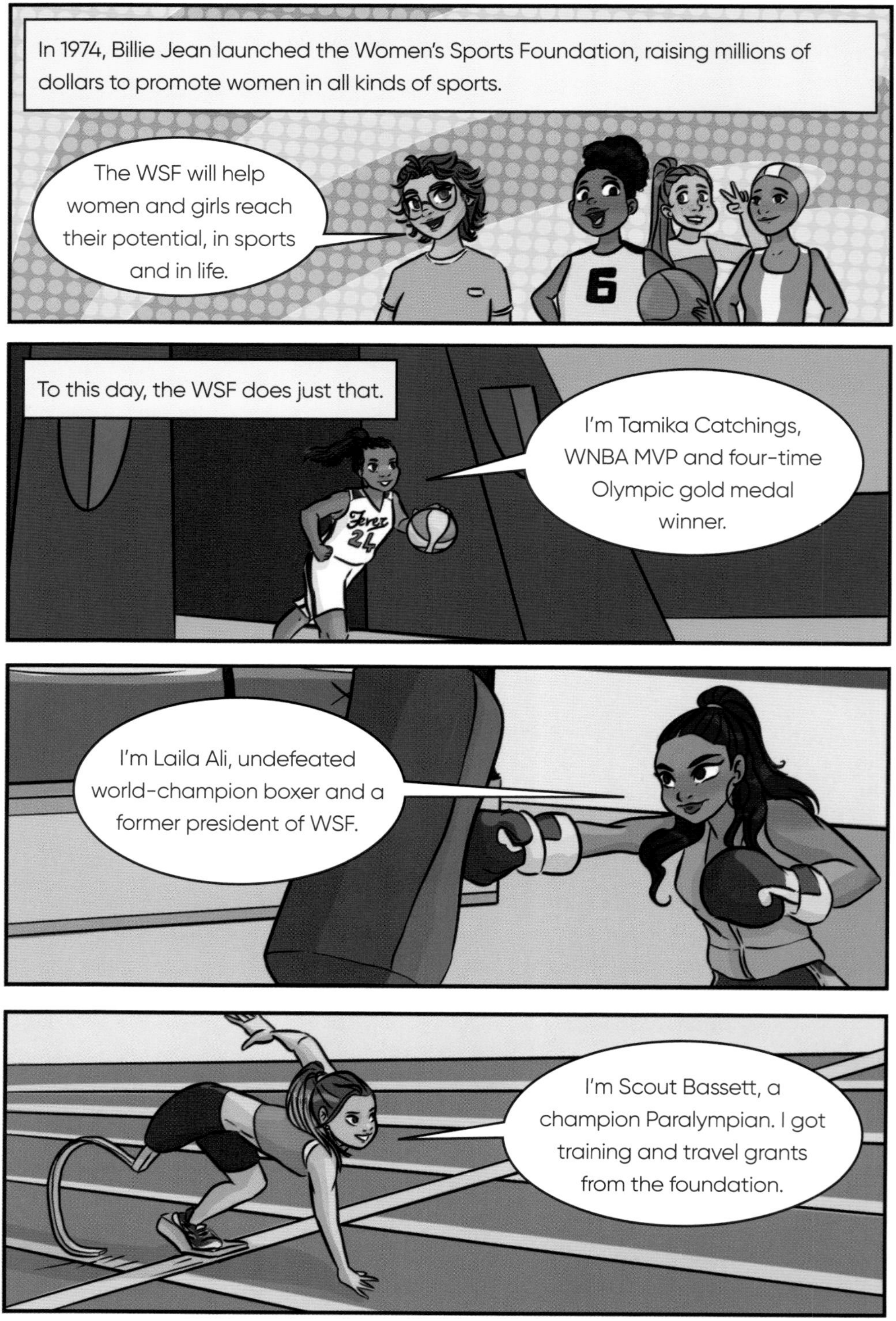
In 1974, Billie Jean launched the Women's Sports Foundation, raising millions of dollars to promote women in all kinds of sports.
The WSF will help women and girls reach their potential, in sports and in life.
To this day, the WSF does just that.
I'm Tamika Catchings, WNBA MVP and four-time Olympic gold medal winner.
I'm Laila Ali, undefeated world-champion boxer and a former president of WSF.
I'm Scout Bassett, a champion Paralympian. I got training and travel grants from the foundation.

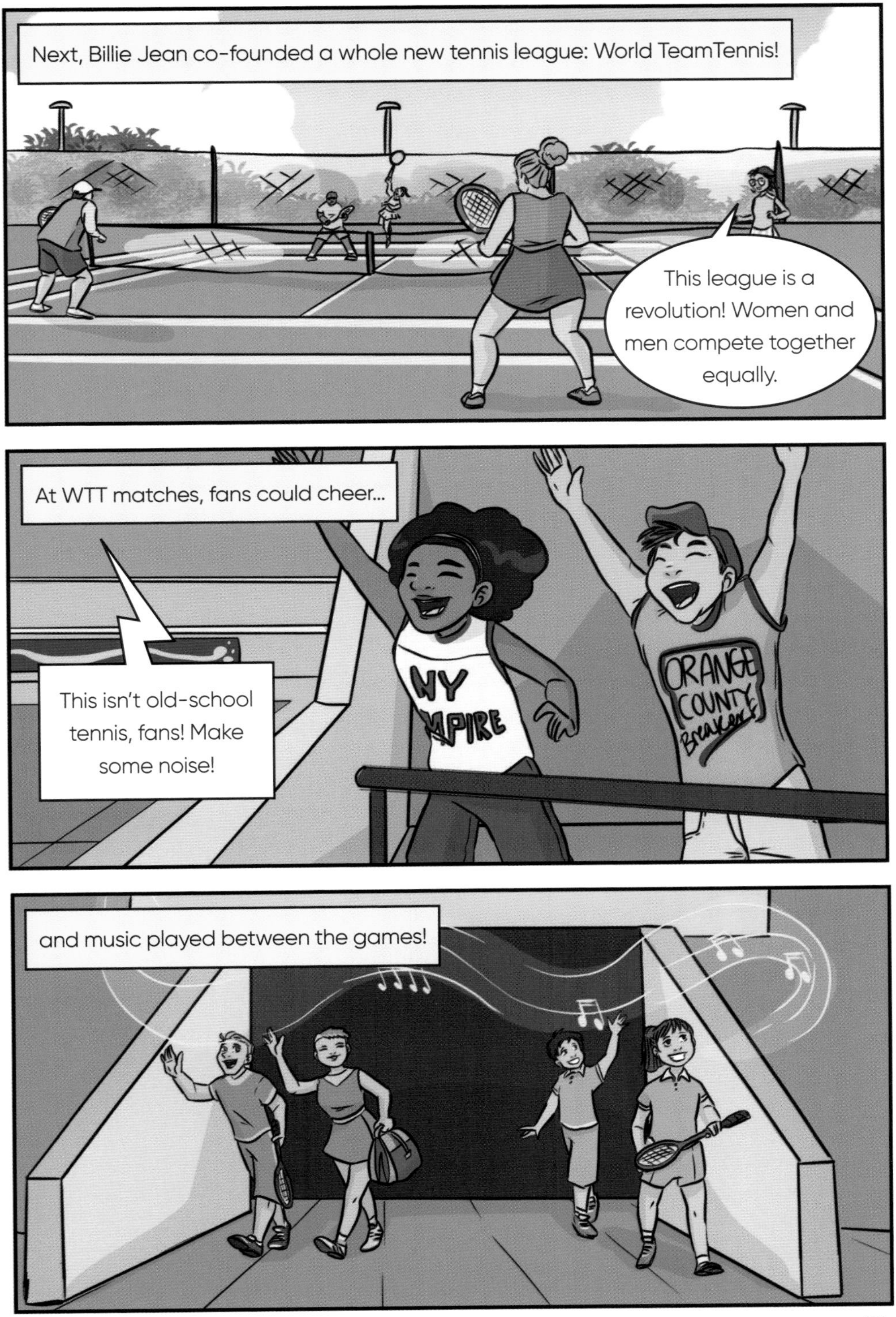
Next, Billie Jean co-founded a whole new tennis league: World TeamTennis!
This league is a revolution! Women and men compete together equally.
At WTT matches, fans could cheer...
This isn't old-school tennis, fans! Make some noise!
NY
ORANGE COUNTY
and music played between the games!

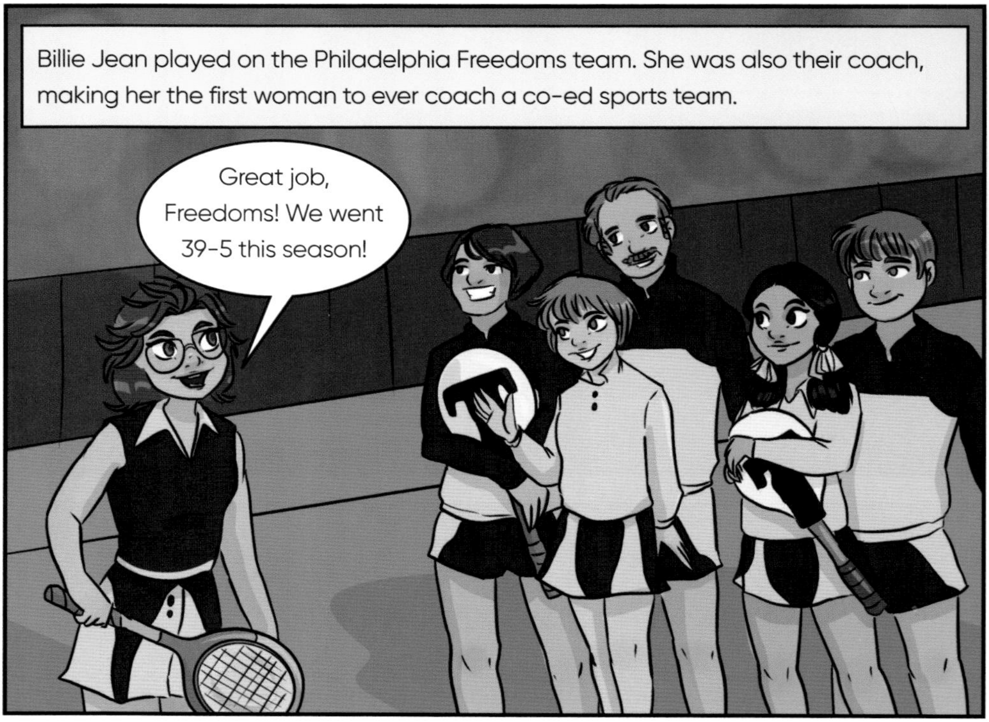
Billie Jean played on the Philadelphia Freedoms team. She was also their coach, making her the first woman to ever coach a co-ed sports team.
Great job, Freedoms! We went 39-5 this season!

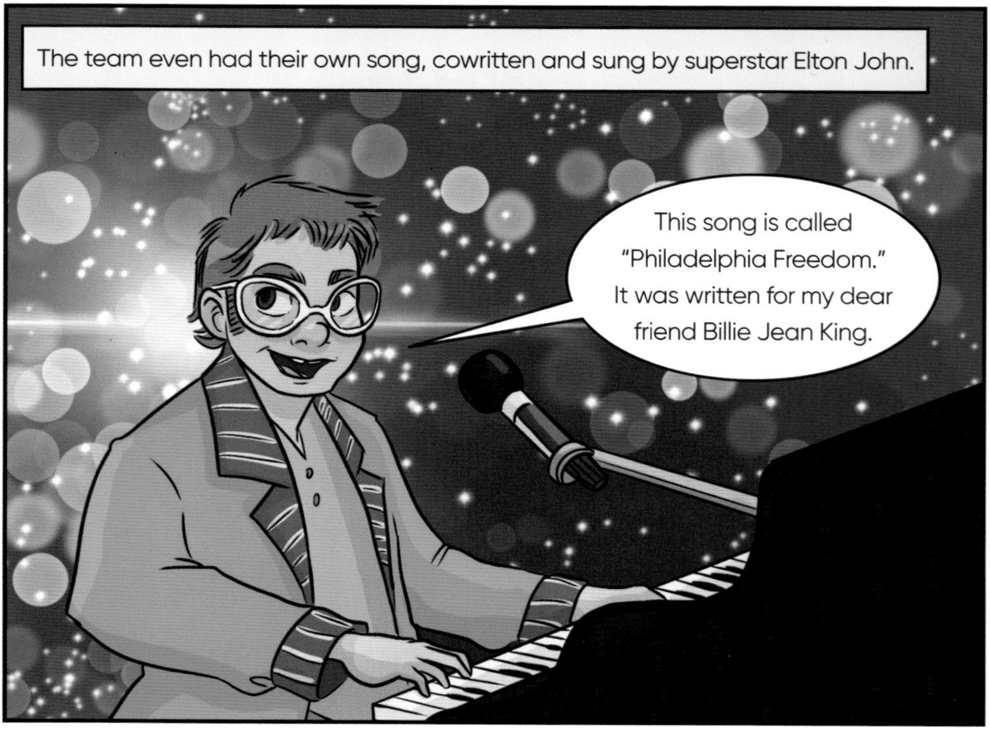
The team even had their own song, cowritten and sung by superstar Elton John.
This song is called "Philadelphia Freedom." It was written for my dear friend Billie Jean King.

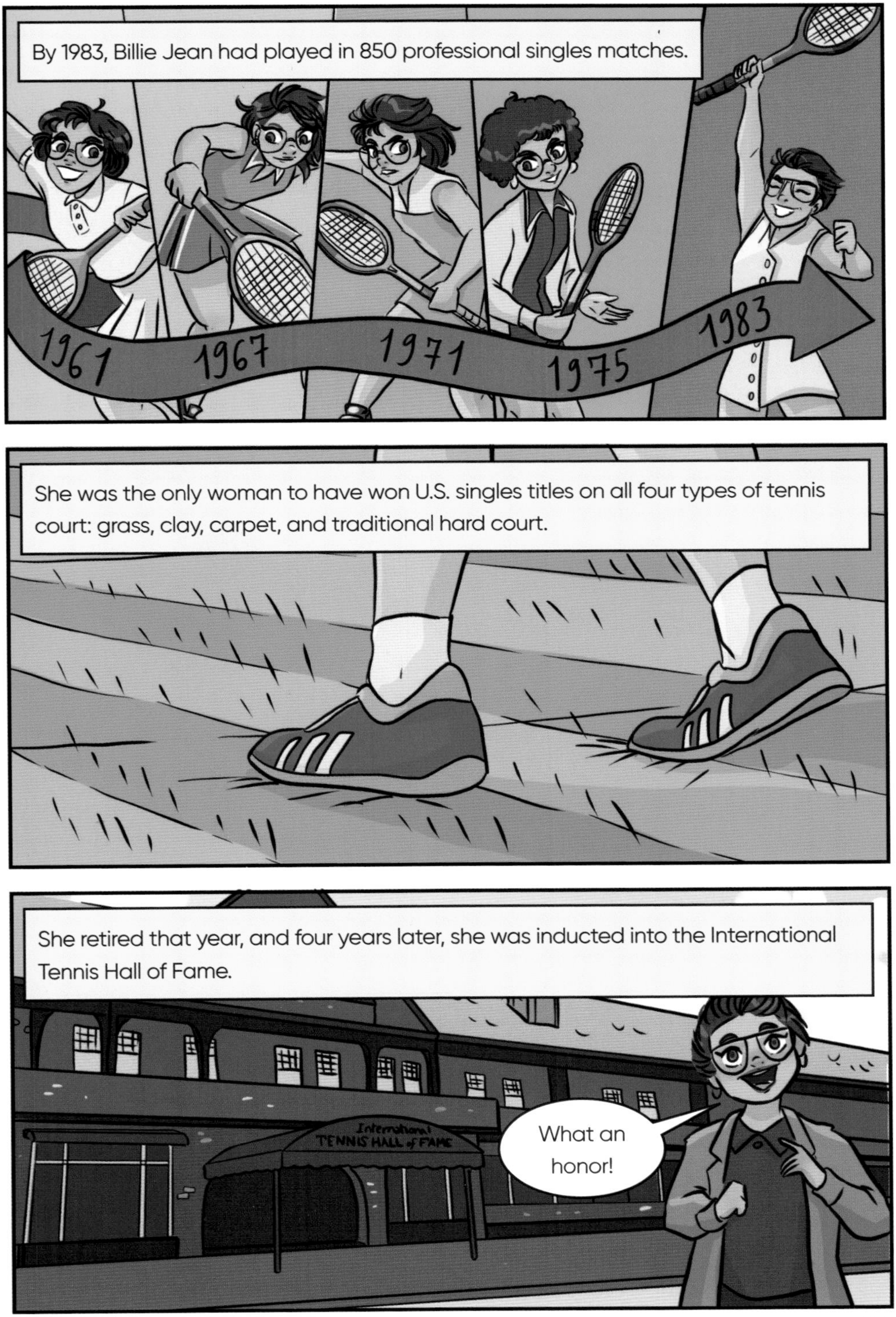
By 1983, Billie Jean had played in 850 professional singles matches.
1961
1967
1971
1975
1983
She was the only woman to have won U.S. singles titles on all four types of tennis court: grass, clay, carpet, and traditional hard court.
She retired that year, and four years later, she was inducted into the International Tennis Hall of Fame.
International TENNIS HALL of FAME
What an honor!

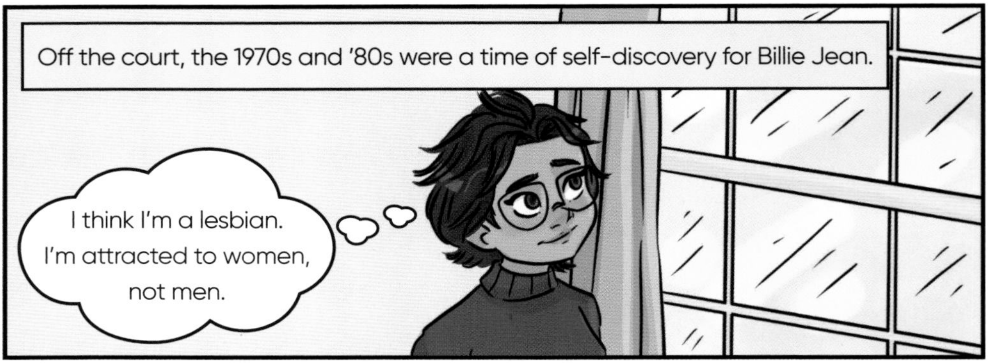
Off the court, the 1970s and '80s were a time of self-discovery for Billie Jean.
I think I'm a lesbian. I'm attracted to women, not men.

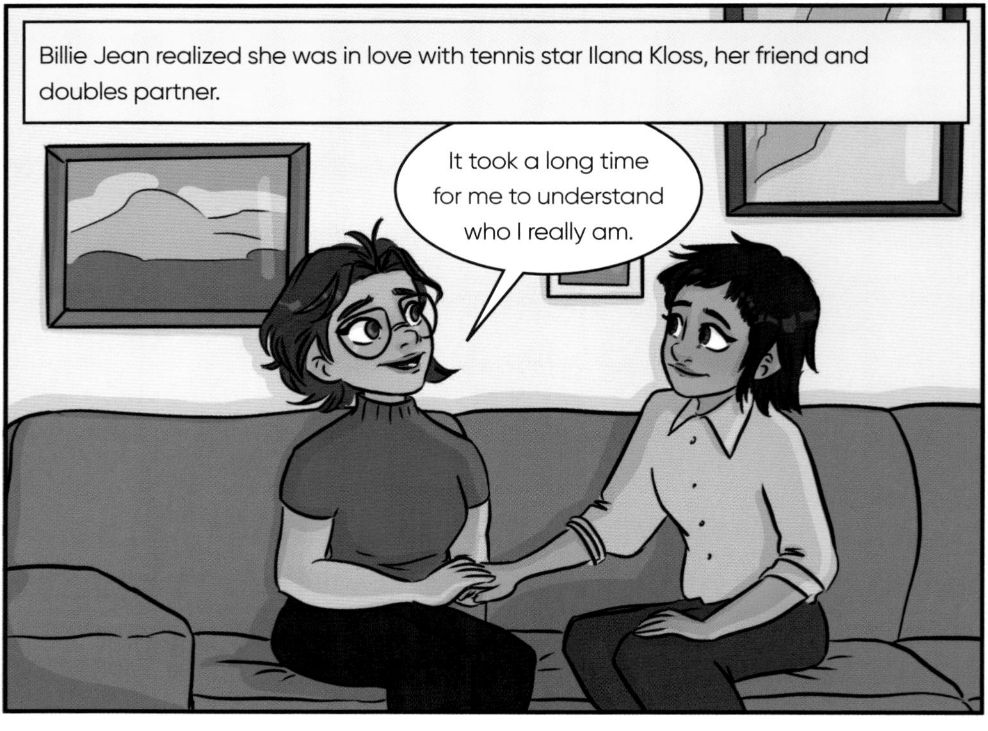
Billie Jean realized she was in love with tennis star Ilana Kloss, her friend and doubles partner.
It took a long time for me to understand who I really am.

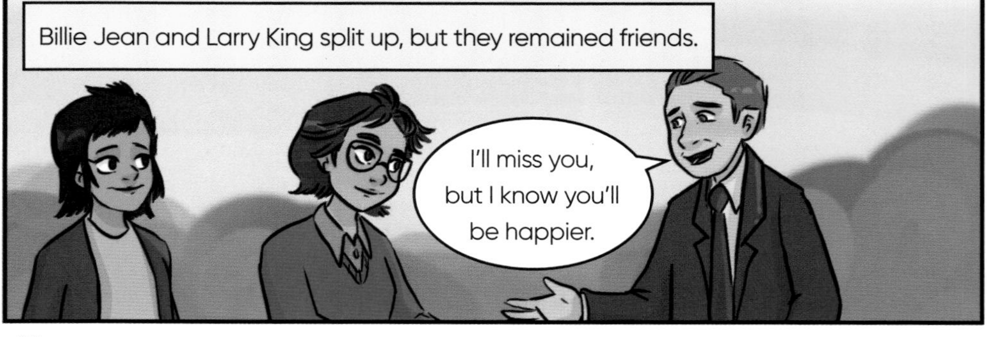
Billie Jean and Larry King split up, but they remained friends.
I'll miss you, but I know you'll be happier.

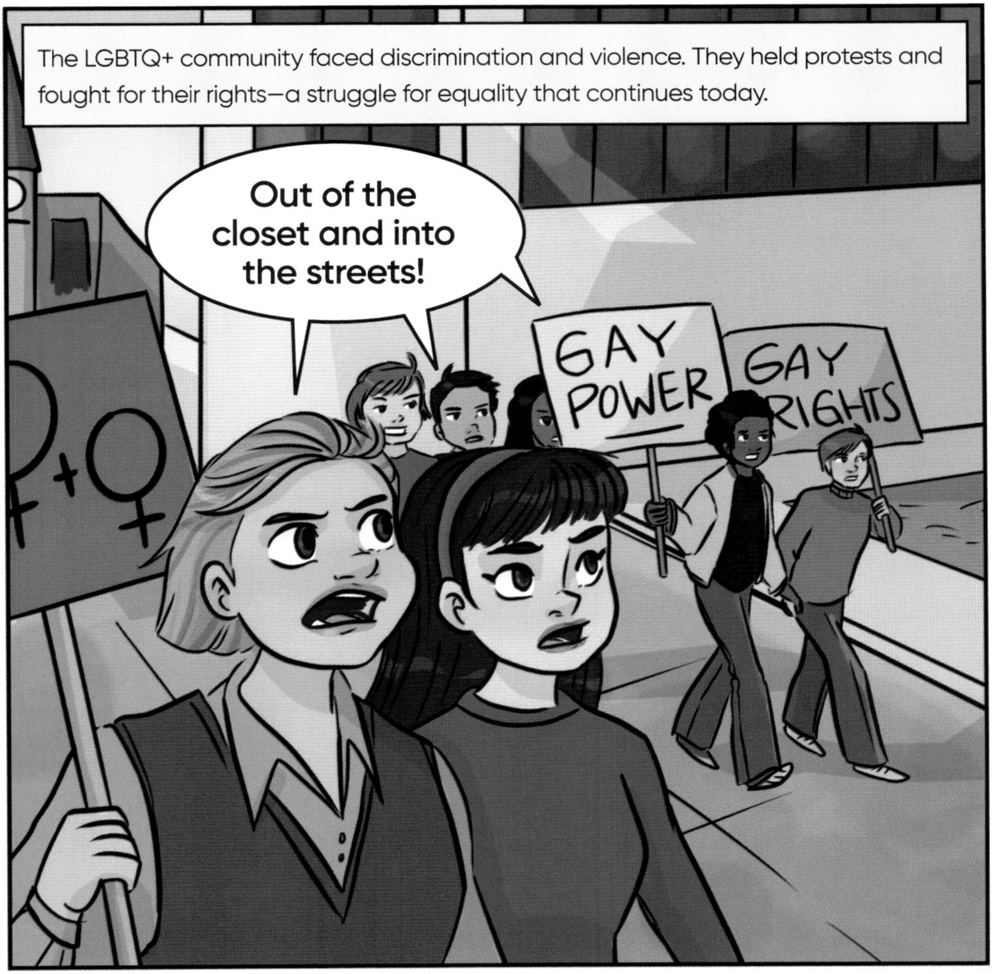
The LGBTQ+ community faced discrimination and violence. They held protests and fought for their rights—a struggle for equality that continues today.
Out of the closet and into the streets!
GAY POWER
GAY RIGHTS

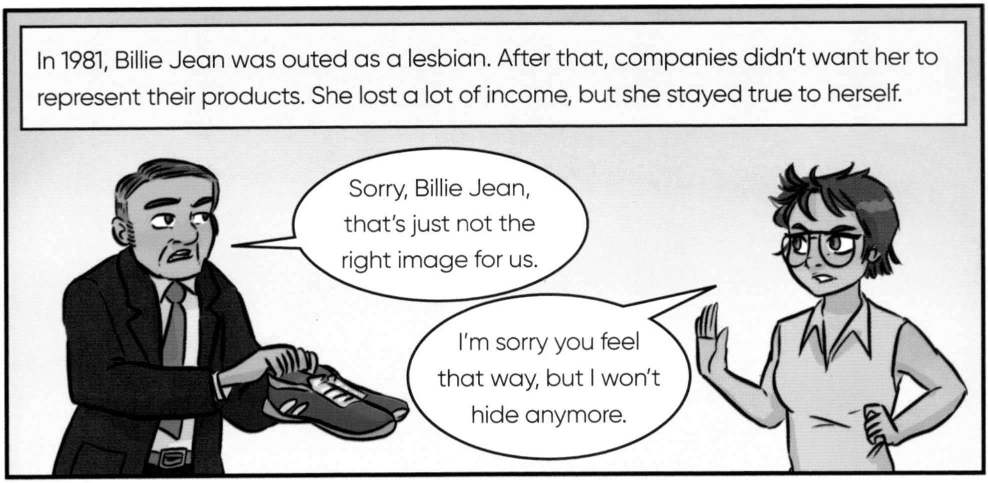
In 1981, Billie Jean was outed as a lesbian. After that, companies didn't want her to represent their products. She lost a lot of income, but she stayed true to herself.
Sorry, Billie Jean, that's just not the right image for us.
I'm sorry you feel that way, but I won't hide anymore.

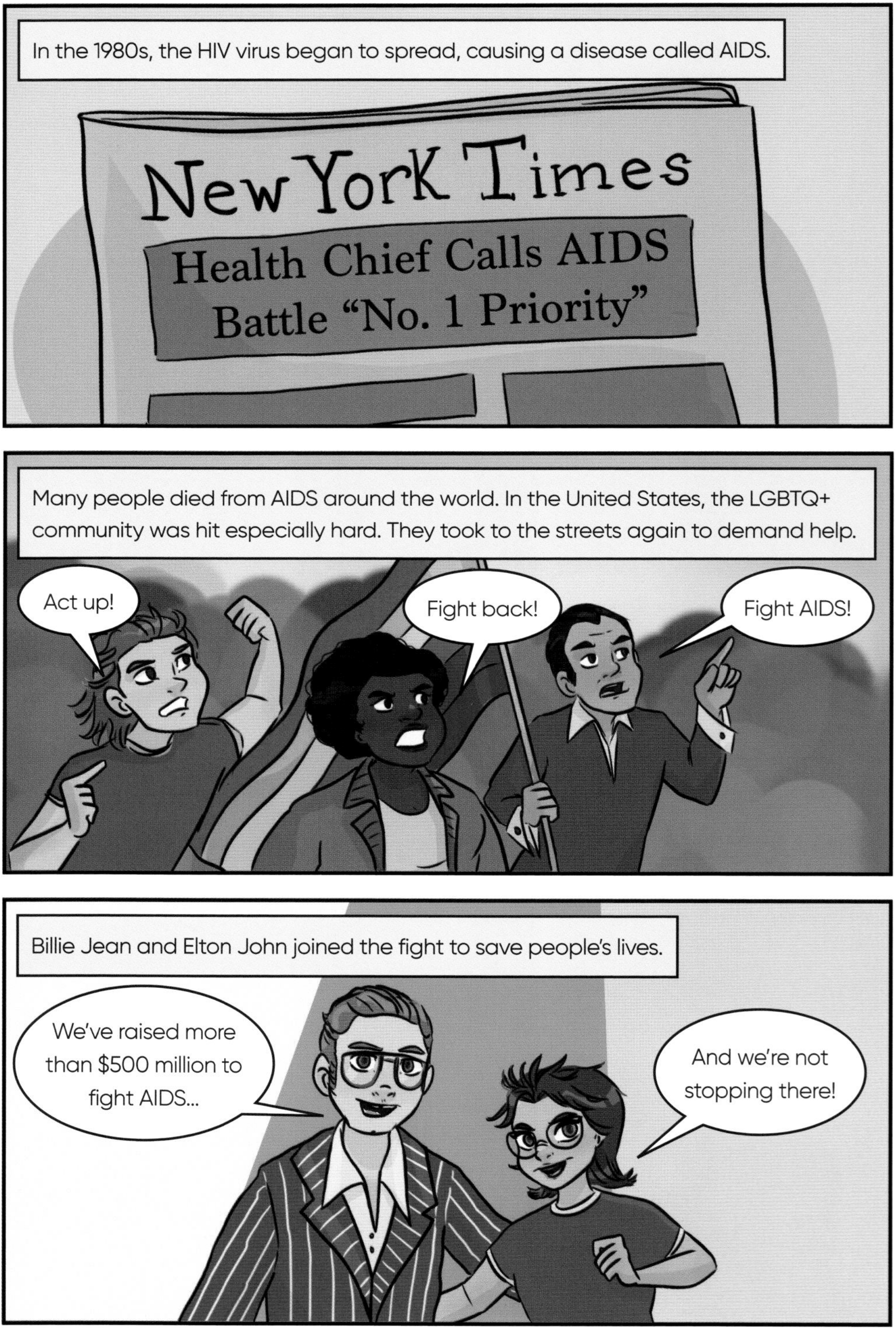
In the 1980s, the HIV virus began to spread, causing a disease called AIDS.
New York Times
Health Chief Calls AIDS Battle "No. 1 Priority"
Many people died from AIDS around the world. In the United States, the LGBTQ+ community was hit especially hard. They took to the streets again to demand help.
Act up!
Fight back!
Fight AIDS!
Billie Jean and Elton John joined the fight to save people's lives.
We've raised more than $500 million to fight AIDS...
And we're not stopping there!

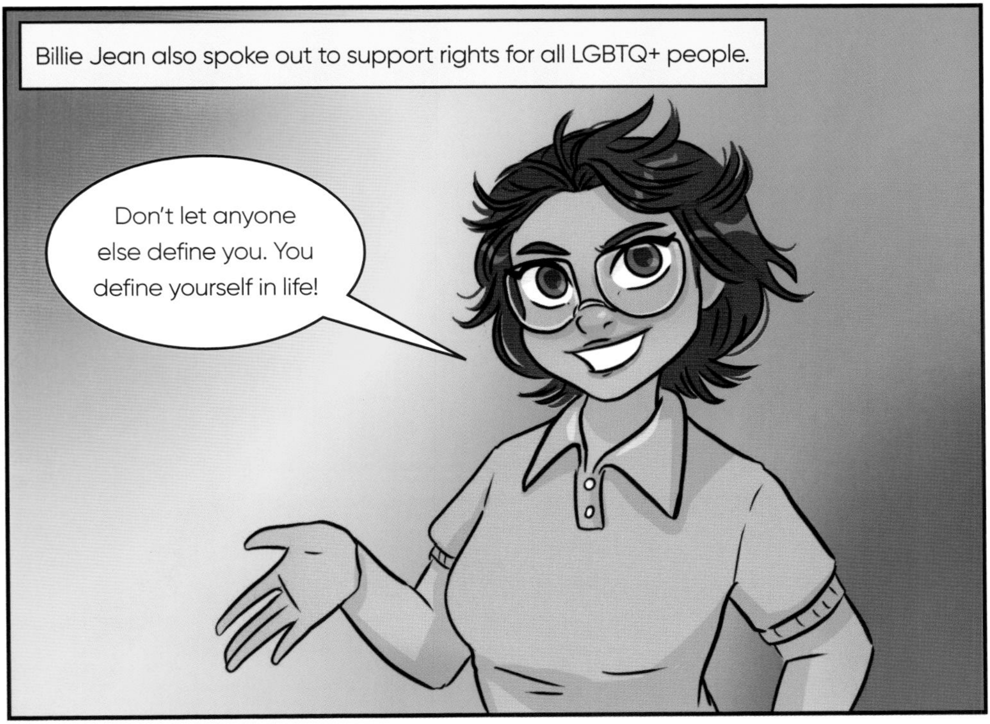
Billie Jean also spoke out to support rights for all LGBTQ+ people.
Don't let anyone else define you. You define yourself in life!

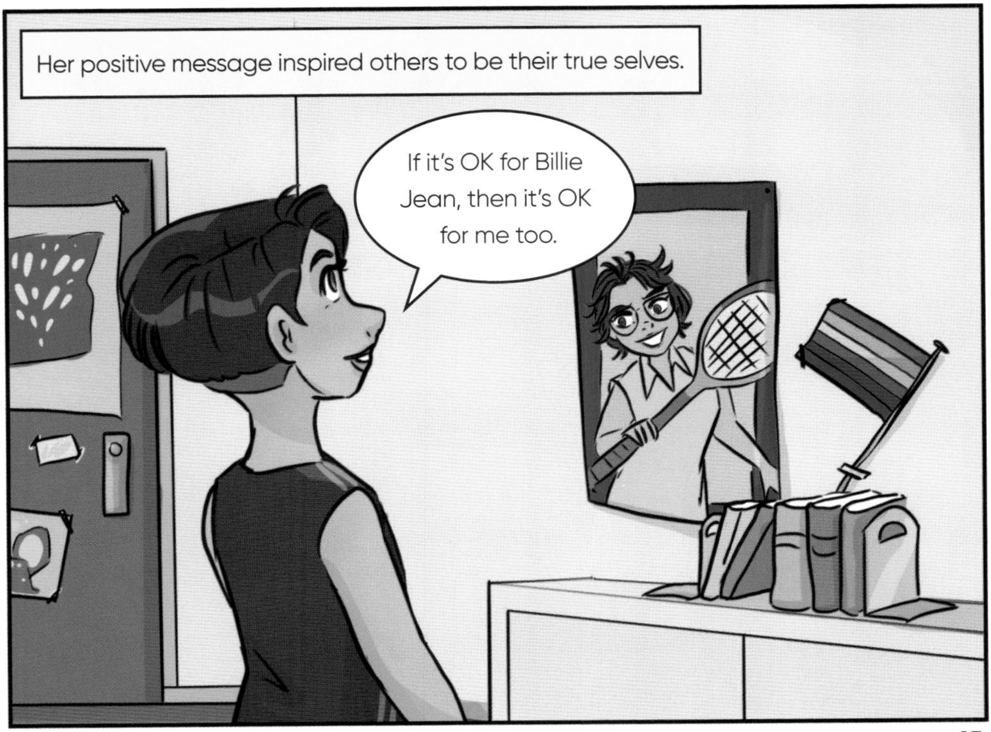
Her positive message inspired others to be their true selves.
If it's OK for Billie Jean, then it's OK for me too.

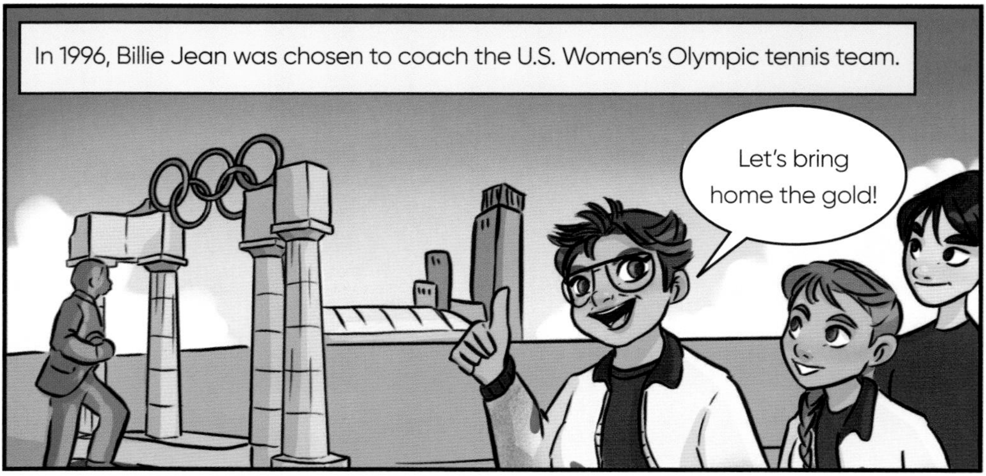
In 1996, Billie Jean was chosen to coach the U.S. Women's Olympic tennis team.
Let's bring home the gold!

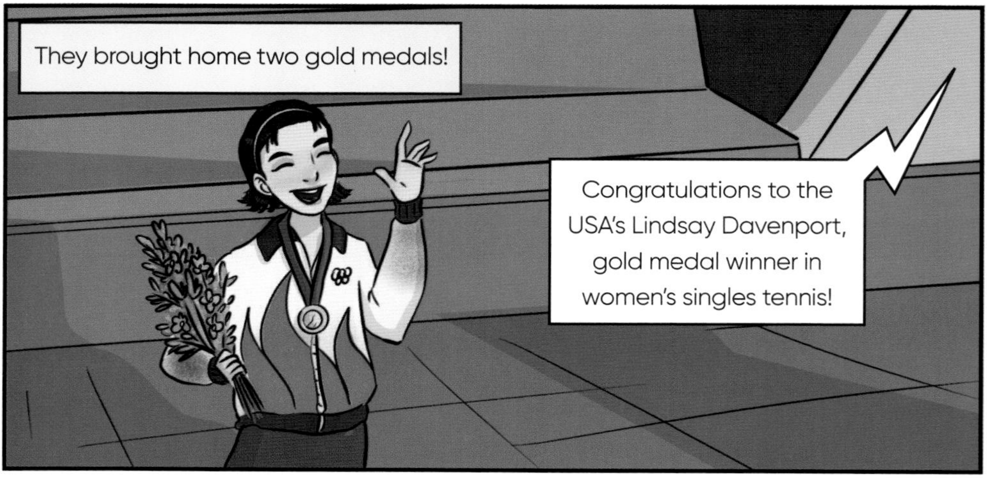
They brought home two gold medals!
Congratulations to the USA's Lindsay Davenport, gold medal winner in women's singles tennis!

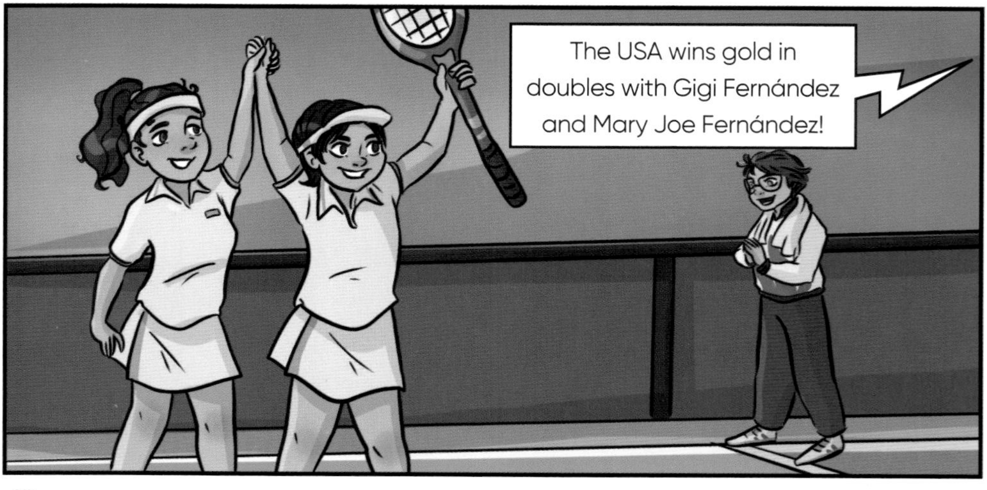
The USA wins gold in doubles with Gigi Fernández and Mary Joe Fernández!

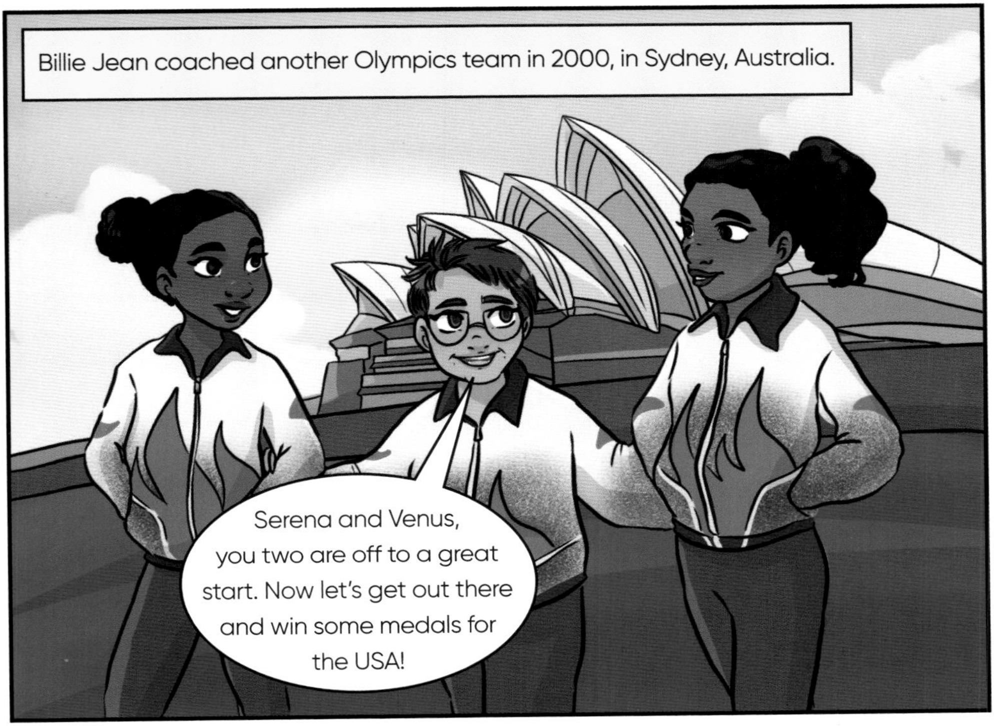
Billie Jean coached another Olympics team in 2000, in Sydney, Australia.
Serena and Venus, you two are off to a great start. Now let's get out there and win some medals for the USA!

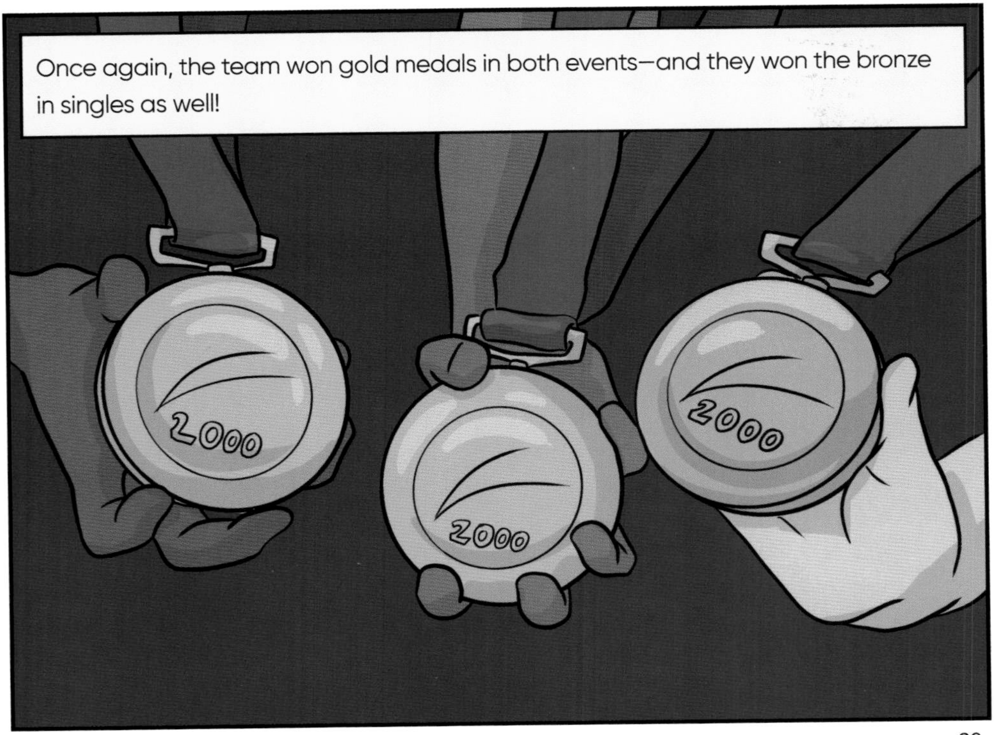
Once again, the team won gold medals in both events—and they won the bronze in singles as well!
2000
2000
2000

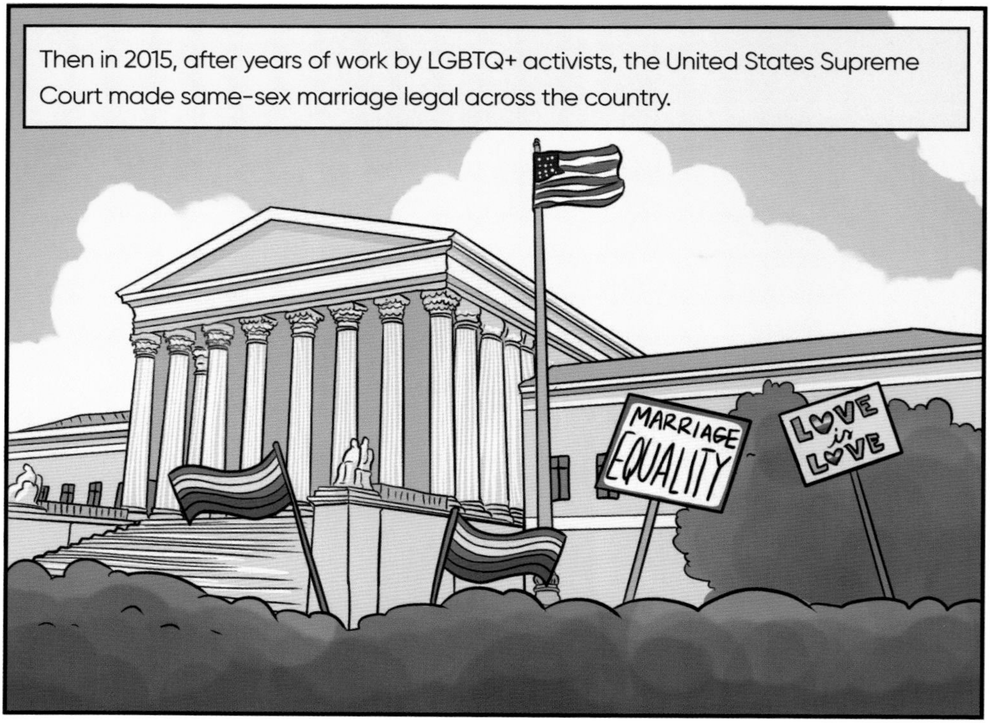
Then in 2015, after years of work by LGBTQ+ activists, the United States Supreme Court made same-sex marriage legal across the country.
MARRIAGE EQUALITY
LOVE is LOVE

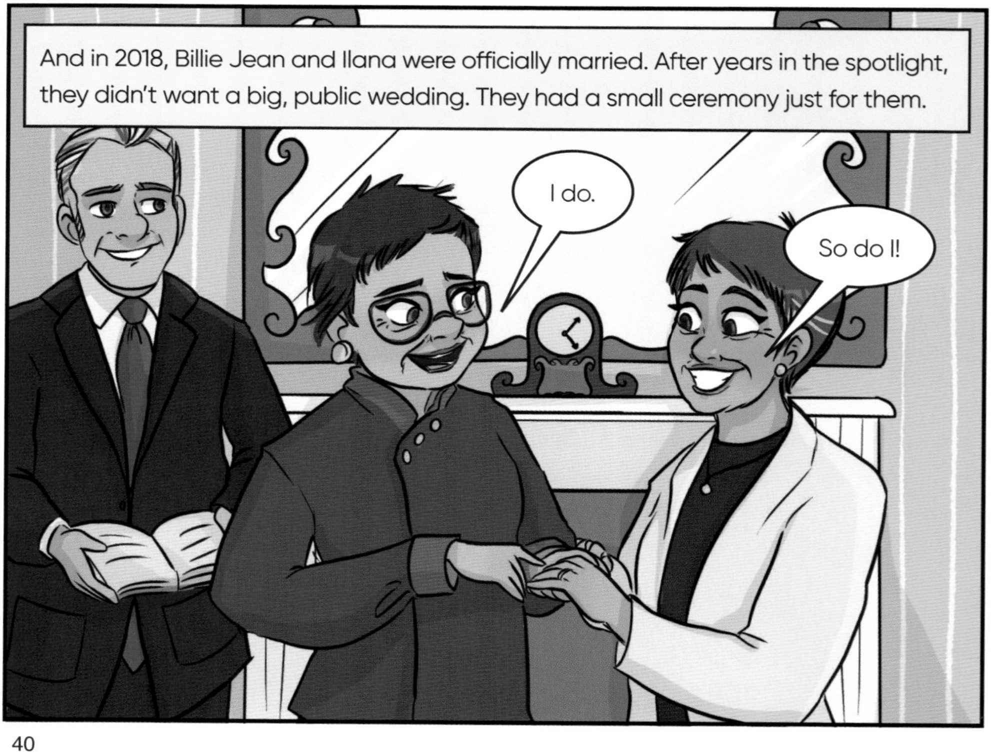
And in 2018, Billie Jean and Ilana were officially married. After years in the spotlight, they didn't want a big, public wedding. They had a small ceremony just for them.
I do.
So do I!

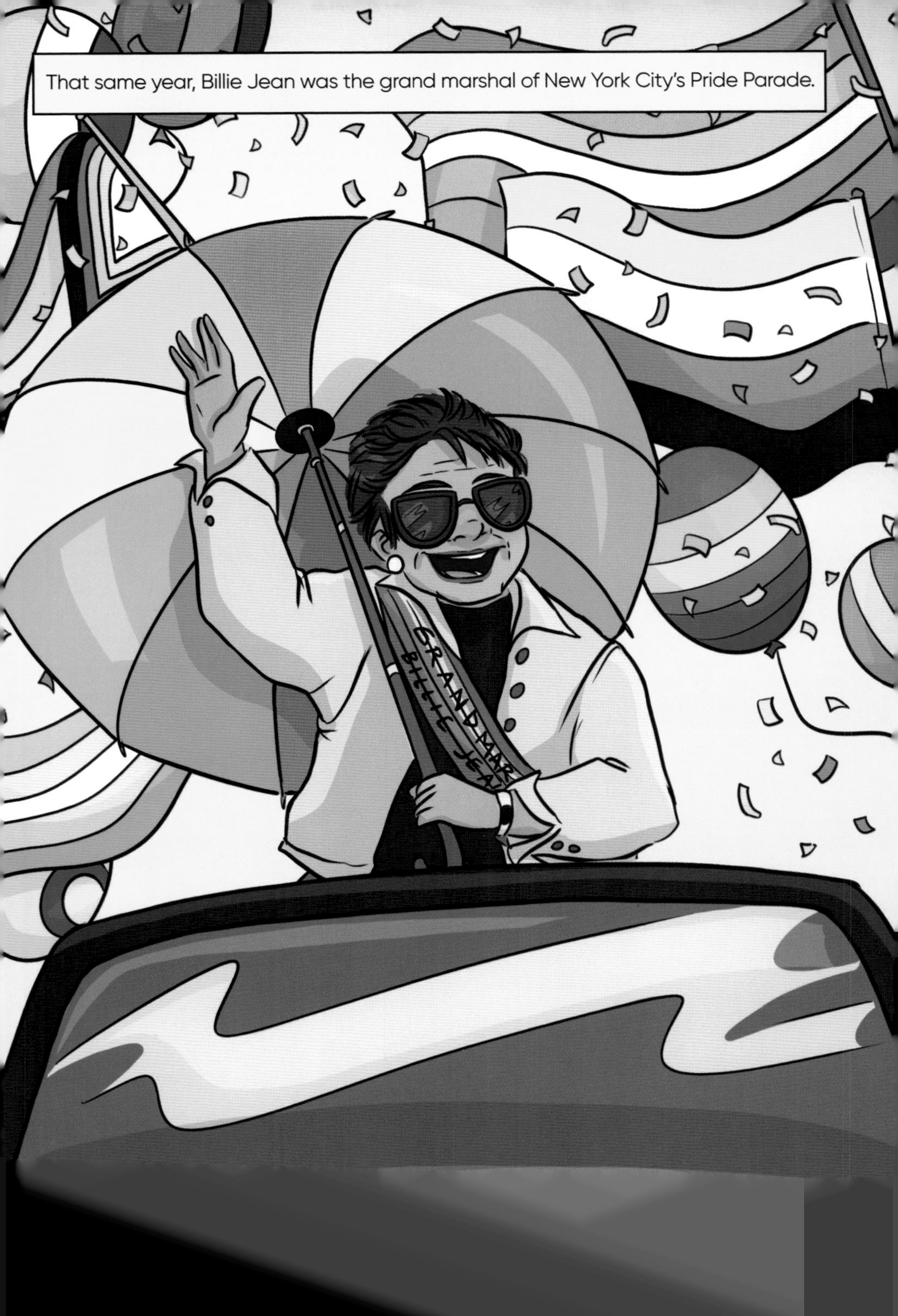
That same year, Billie Jean was the grand marshal of New York City's Pride Parade.

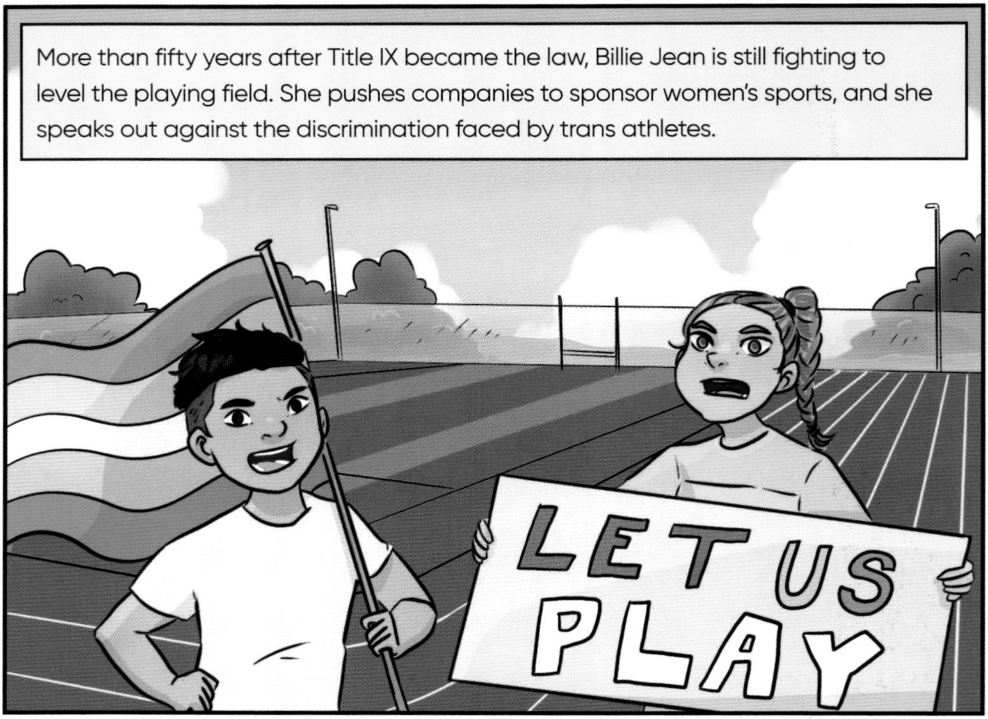
More than fifty years after Title IX became the law, Billie Jean is still fighting to level the playing field. She pushes companies to sponsor women's sports, and she speaks out against the discrimination faced by trans athletes.
LET US PLAY

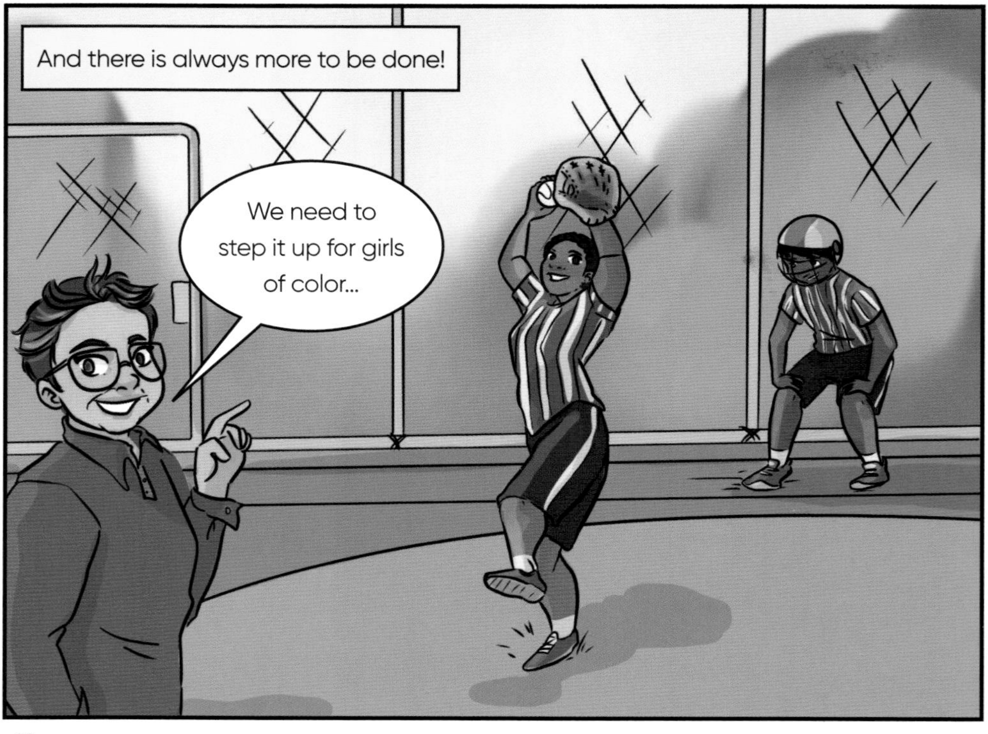
And there is always more to be done!
We need to step it up for girls of color...

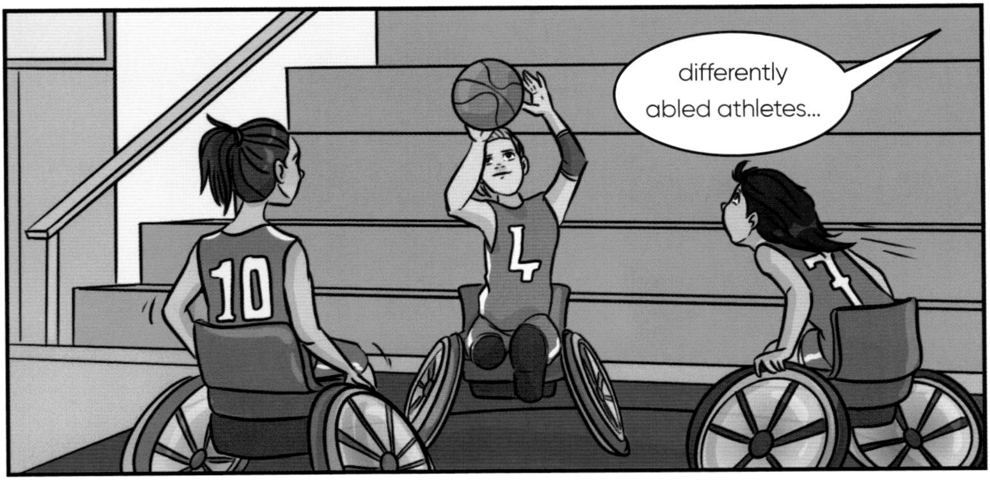
differently abled athletes...

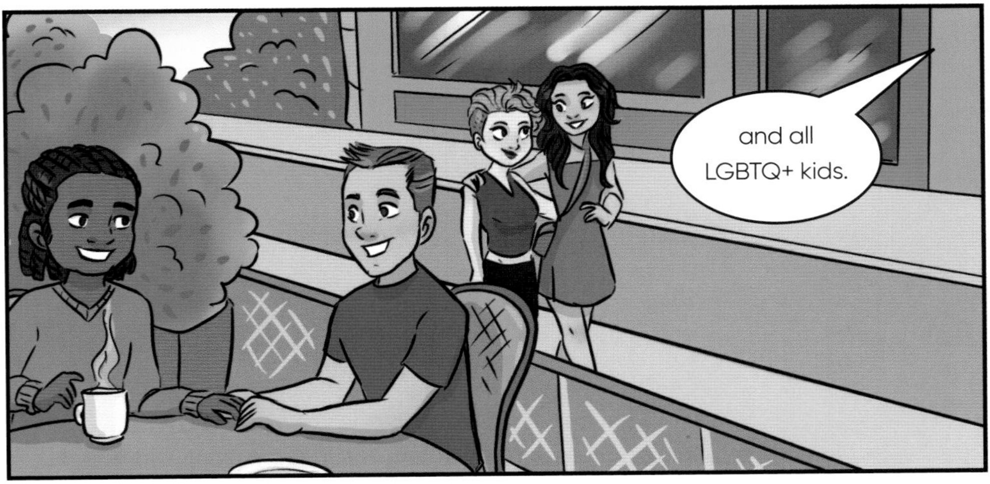
and all LGBTQ+ kids.

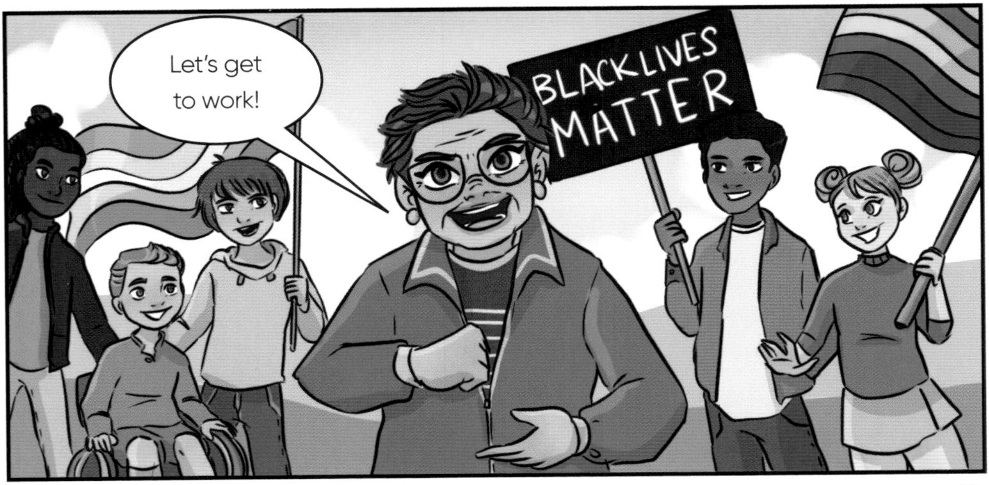
Let's get to work!
BLACK LIVES MATTER

Billie Jean has received many honors throughout her life, including:

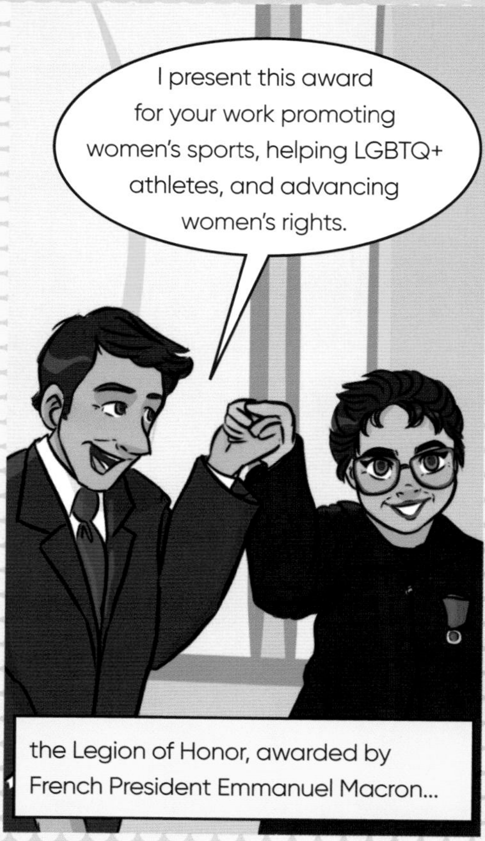
I present this award for your work promoting women's sports, helping LGBTQ+ athletes, and advancing women's rights.
the Legion of Honor, awarded by French President Emmanuel Macron...

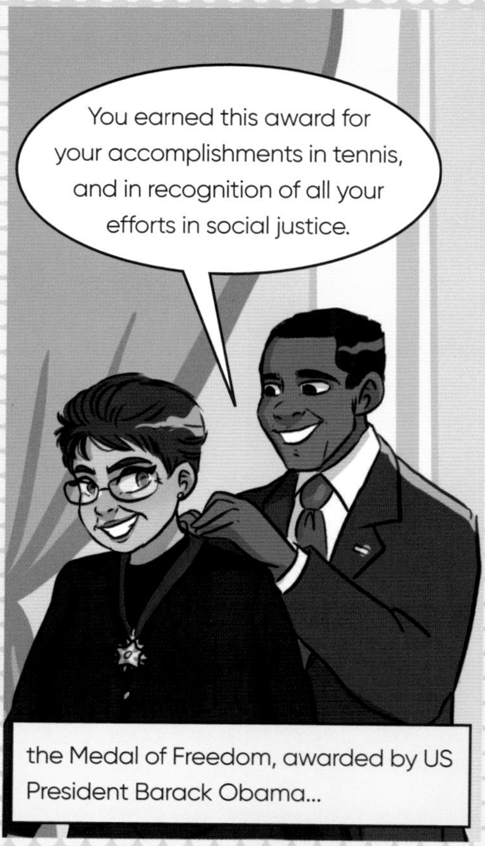
You earned this award for your accomplishments in tennis, and in recognition of all your efforts in social justice.
the Medal of Freedom, awarded by US President Barack Obama...

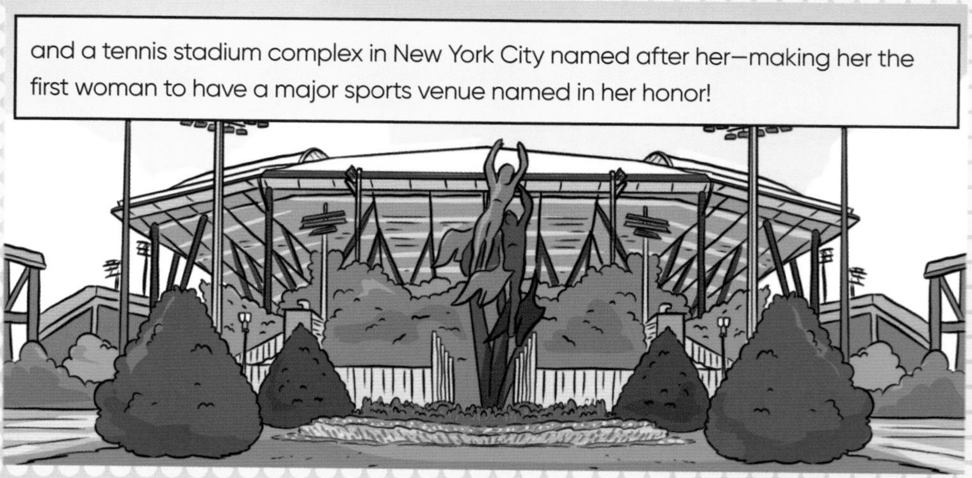
and a tennis stadium complex in New York City named after her—making her the first woman to have a major sports venue named in her honor!

Donna Tapellini is a writer and attorney who lives in New Jersey with her wife, their goldendoodle, and their three cats. She's not much of a tennis player, but she loves pickleball. She also enjoys kayaking, reading, working in her garden, and bird-watching. She's always up for an adventure, but sometimes the perfect day involves a simple game of catch on the beach with her dog.

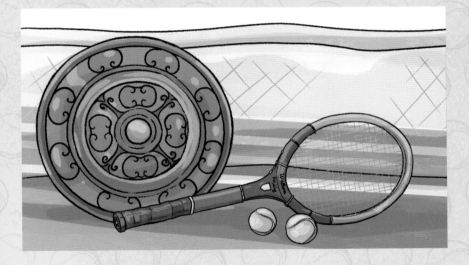

Maria Lia Malandrino is an illustrator based in Torino, Italy, who grew up reading fantasy books and comics. She has worked as a graphic designer, animator, and concept artist, and has always felt compelled to tell stories through images. In her free time, she likes to row on the river that flows through her hometown, hike with her young family and dog, and play strategy games and role-playing games.

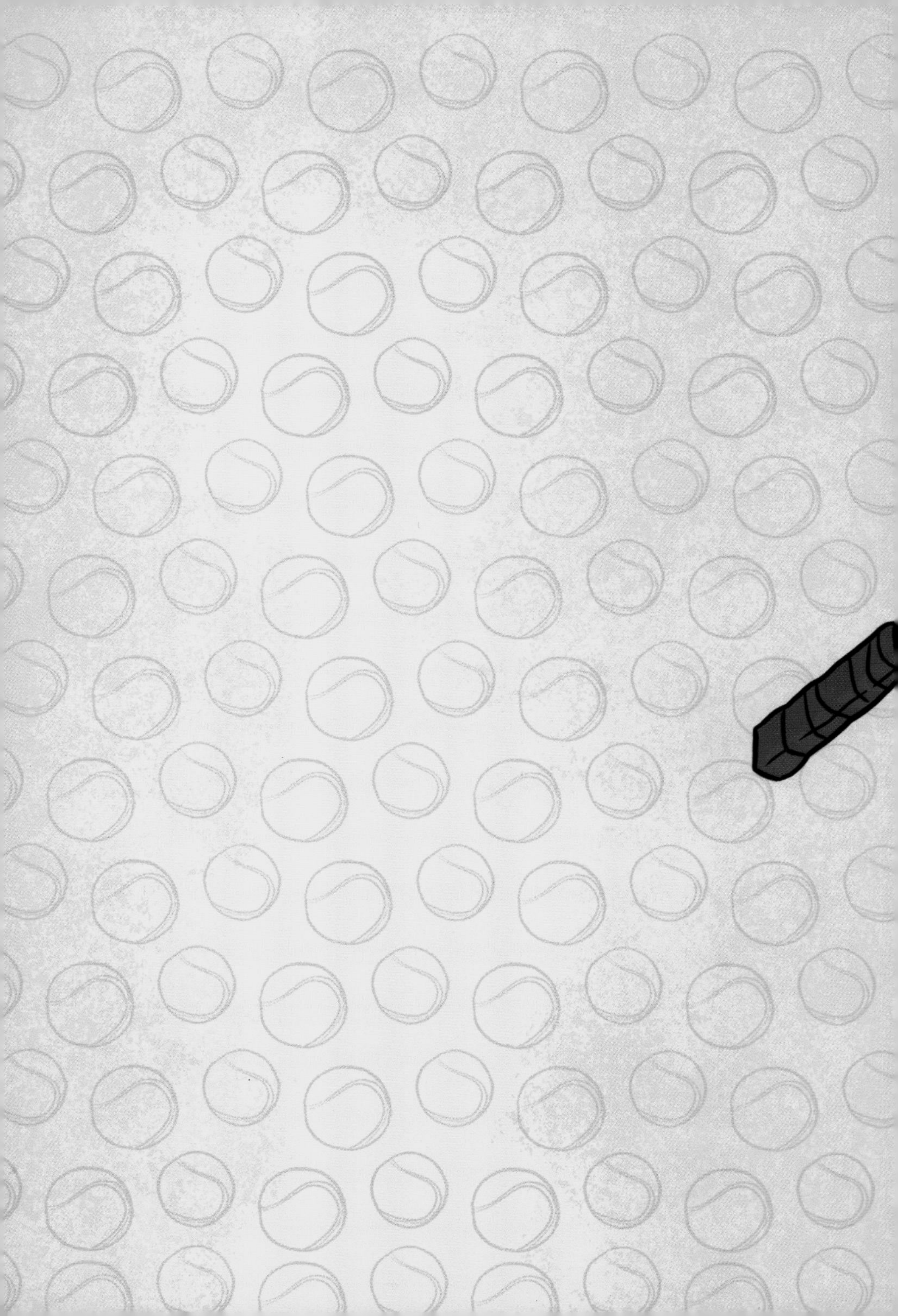